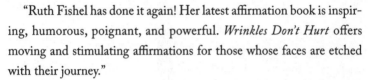

Prais...
Wrinkles D...

"Ruth Fishel has done it again! Her latest affirmation book is inspiring, humorous, poignant, and powerful. *Wrinkles Don't Hurt* offers moving and stimulating affirmations for those whose faces are etched with their journey."

—**Rokelle Lerner**, author of *Affirmations for Adult Children of Alcoholics, Affirmations for the Inner Child, Living in the Comfort Zone,* and *The Object of My Affection is in My Reflection: Coping with Narcissists*

"In *Wrinkles Don't Hurt*, Ruth Fishel allows her readers to embark on the journey of aging with a refreshing vision of the elder years as a time of celebration and liberation, a time to set new goals, dream new dreams, to grow into ourselves emotionally and spiritually, and extend a helping hand to others. Ruth presents aging as a time of limitless opportunities and choices rather than merely a time of limits and losses."

—**Jane Middelton-Moz**, author of *Values from the Front Porch* and *Shame and Guilt: Masters of Disguise*

"Ruth Fishel has hit another home run. *Wrinkles Don't Hurt* is an excellent book. It's soothing, thought provoking, discerning and pleasantly quiet in all the right places. The drawings are perfect too. They tickle one's fancy and make the book a treasure to have, to read and to give to others. I feel blessed to have had a chance to read it."

—**Karen Casey**, author of *Each Day a New Beginning*

"Ruth Fishel's book reminds us, with a series of daily quotes, reflections, and meditation practices, that mindfulness is indeed the best medicine. As we enter the golden years of our lives, we all have a unique opportunity to live more fully by dwelling on what we have and not on what we are losing. So embrace your wrinkles and this book as a gentle reminder of the preciousness of life. The art of mindfulness will offer you the best ways to soothe and heal the mind, body, and spirit. As you practice these simple methods of stopping and calming, you will understand how the meaning of life comes in small doses and is always available to us moment by moment."

—**Jerry Braza, Ph.D.**, Dharma teacher,
Thich Nhat Hanh lineage, and author of
The Seeds of Love: Growing Mindful Relationships

"*Wrinkles Don't Hurt* is another great contribution from Ruth Fishel. It contains gentle reminders to seize the day, reinforces that we are not alone, and quietly provides motivation. It is one of those books that touches and teaches the soul. I thank her for reminding us about the little things that have the greatest impact on who we are and what we believe."

—**Robert J. Ackerman, Ph.D.**, author of *Perfect Daughters*
and *Silent Sons*, Professor and Director, Human Services
Program University of South Carolina, Beaufort

Wrinkles Don't Hurt

Wrinkles Don't Hurt

Daily Meditations on the Joy of Aging Mindfully

Ruth Fishel, Author of the bestselling *Time for Joy*

Illustrations by Bonny Van de Kamp

Health Communications, Inc.
Deerfield Beach, Florida

www.hcibooks.com

Library of Congress Cataloging-in-Publication Data

Fishel, Ruth, 1935–
    Wrinkles don't hurt : daily affirmations on the joys of aging mindfully / Ruth Fishel.
        p. cm.
    ISBN-13: 978-0-7573-1590-9 (pbk.)
    ISBN-10: 0-7573-1590-9 (pbk.)
    ISBN-13: 978-0-7573-9162-0 (e-book)
    ISBN-10: 0-7573-9162-1 (e-book)
    1. Aging—Miscellanea.   2. Affirmations.   3. Meditation.   I. Title.
    HQ1061.F527 2011
    305.26—dc23

                                                                            2011038495

Publisher: Health Communications, Inc.
            3201 S.W. 15th Street
            Deerfield Beach, FL 33442–8190

Cover illustration by Bonny Van de Kamp
Cover and interior designs by Lawna Patterson Oldfield

To Nathan J. Haase (1901–1994),

my father, who taught me to swim, ski, ride horseback,

fly kites, ride a bike, to stop and marvel at rainbows and mirages,

to take time to enjoy nature, and to always root for the Red Sox.

When I was ten he told me that someday I would

appreciate simply sitting and looking at the water.

I do, and I wish he were here so I could tell him.

I have a sense that he might know.

With Gratitude

There are so many people to thank for helping to make this book possible.

I want to begin with Sandy Bierig, my life partner of thirty-seven years at the time of this writing, who has always made the space in our lives for my work, and edited the first version of this book and all my other books before sending it to the publisher.

To Bonny Van de Kamp, the creator of all the wonderful drawings found in *Wrinkles Don't Hurt, Time for Joy,* and many of my other books. Bonny's enthusiasm, talent, sense of humor, and huge, loving heart has been a gift in my life for over twenty years.

A deep bow to Joseph Goldstein, Larry Rosenberg, Sharon Salzberg, and my first meditation teachers: Christina Feldman, Narayan Lieberman, and many others along the way; as well as my current teachers Fred Eppsteiner, Joanne Friday, and Bill Menza.

To the many people who have contributed their wisdom and energy on their pages inside.

To Allison Janse, editor at Health Communications, Inc., who is a joy to work with.

To Peter Vegso, publisher and owner of Health Communications, Inc., who has always been ready to take a chance on my new ideas.

To all the scientists and researchers who have studied the brain and have discovered how we can change our lives by changing our thoughts and how mindfulness helps to make these changes possible.

To my daughters, Debbie Boisseau and Judy Fishel, for their love and support along the way.

And last but not least, to Bill W. and Dr. Bob, without whom I would not be alive.

Introduction

Dear Readers,

Many years ago my publisher suggested that I write a daily meditation book geared toward older people. I thought about it, tried it, and couldn't make it flow. I didn't have specific words within me for older people. Some years earlier I had written *Time for Joy*, a daily meditation book for all ages. There was no difference, I thought, between what I would say to a younger or middle-aged person and what I would say to someone older. Inspiration is inspiration no matter how young or old you are!

One evening, while we were having dinner at our house, friends asked if we would like to go kayaking and canoeing with them in the spring. My partner immediately said she wasn't up to it while I enthusiastically answered yes! I had wanted to try kayaking for a long time and thought it would be great fun. I overheard my partner whisper something.

"What did she say?" I asked.

One friend laughed and responded: "She said, 'Ruth doesn't know how old she is!'"

The truth was, back then I didn't identify my age as old. And I don't identify with the age I am now as old. I knew I was getting older but I felt relatively healthy and capable and I had good energy, as I do today, although it was true that I couldn't do all the things I could have done ten or twenty years earlier.

That day I thought, *Maybe there is a book for me to write after all.* While inspiration is the same for all ages, there are many other specific differences. As we grow up, our issues change. Although our inner spirit ideally continues to grow freer and more spiritually connected, our physical bodies develop limitations which prevent us from doing everything we would like to or think we can do. Losses, limitations, changing times, pain, and diminished energy all sneak up on us. How we look at life changes. What was important a few years earlier might be less important today.

It is amazing to think that the average life expectancy in 1900 was in the 40s. Today it is between 75 and 80, depending on whether you are a woman or man. So while we are healthier physically for many more years because of new medical information, we are just now understanding how our brains can be healthy as well. Only within the past 30 or so years have scientists discovered neuroplasticity, a term used to describe the brain changes that occur in response to our experience. We now know that new connections and new neurons can form, and many experiments have proven that the practice of mindfulness meditation produces actual changes in the brain. Until this discovery, it was thought that our brains were hard-wired, that they couldn't change once we arrived at a certain age.

It is very exciting news that we can be physically and mentally healthier and maintain our memory for much longer and, all in all, live a happier, more productive life. Whether you are 30 or 90, you can benefit from the daily inspirations in *Wrinkles Don't Hurt*.

As a daily meditator for over 30 years, I have experienced firsthand everything this book says is possible. This book will guide you, day by day, to be fully present in each moment while letting go of your fears, doubts, and insecurities.

I am very excited to have you join me on this wonderful path that can bring you the joy of aging mindfully!

With love and peace,
Ruth Fishel
Ellenton, Florida
October, 2011

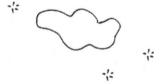

JANUARY

Today I am letting my life flow
. . . mindfully.

Today I am making no plans.
  If I am lucky I might see a monarch
  butterfly resting lightly on a blossom
or get in touch with a truth deep within
    my soul
or even stub my toe or get
    caught in the rain!

I might see the wonder of a
    rainbow or stay inside and watch
    the snow.

I might return the smile of a stranger
    and feel my heart open
or help someone even older than myself
    across the street.
I might do nothing more than watch the sun
    rise and fall and yes, watch everything in
    between from my window.

Today I am letting my life flow . . . mindfully.

How Do We Practice Mindful Meditation?

Meditation is really very simple. Sit either in a crossed-leg position on a cushion, on a meditation bench, or in a chair, wherever you are most comfortable. Sit with your back as straight as possible, with your eyes closed very gently, or look down at a 45-degree angle. Begin by being mindful of your breathing. Feel your breath going in and coming out of your nose. You can also watch your chest as it rises and falls and your stomach as it fills and empties.

It's normal for thoughts to come in, your body to itch or hurt, or for you to become impatient. Simply notice whatever comes up that takes you away from your breathing and return to your breath, without any judgment. The more you practice, the more peaceful you become. Practice this for the minimum of 20 minutes every day. As you develop this practice each day, you will be able to bring this mindful awareness into other areas of your day.

It feels so good to begin my day connecting spiritually
with the practice of mindfulness. I am bringing
peace and an open heart to the rest of my day.

time for reflections

As we grow older there are many things we can do to make our aging more about joy rather than about what is wrong in our lives. Yes, it is true that we may have aches and pains and most likely some memory failure. And yes, there will be changes and losses. But if we allow it, if we make the choice to move in a more spiritual, positive, and compassionate direction, we can create a life filled with happiness. We can grow in wisdom. We can give to others what we have learned from our own experiences. We can come from an open heart and live a rich and meaningful life.

I pray for the wisdom and desire to live
a rich and meaningful life and to
continue to give to others.

"How old would you be if you didn't
know how old you were?"

—*Satchel Paige*

When we're young we might think 30 is old. If we hold on to that thought and take it as our reality, we will dread turning 30. Others might dread turning 40 or 50 or whatever age you think of as old. Unfortunately, we have a preconceived vision of what that old age means, and we think of ourselves as being old when we reach it. I know young people at 70 and old people at 50. Age actually has nothing to do with it. So if we can let go of all our ideas about how it will feel to reach certain ages, we stand a good chance of growing older without anticipating the worst or having fears around aging. We can just be, living one day at a time, and let life take us where it will. We need not label how old we are with stories we made up when we were younger!

*It feels so good to let go of my ideas of young
and old and just be who I am today.*

> "I have known a great many troubles, but
> most of them never happened."
>
> —*Mark Twain*

I remember a time many years ago when I saw a person being pushed in a wheelchair and I thought, with great fear, *Who will there be to push my wheelchair?* It was a very traumatic moment for me. I remember asking a young friend if she would be there for me if I needed her and she promised she would. I don't know where she is today, but maybe I should find her!

I went through another period when I worried about lack of money, getting sick, even losing my mind. I even pictured myself in the poorhouse (are there such things anymore?), lying on a mattress on the floor, in a large room with mattresses lined up everywhere. Now, after years of mindfulness, fearful thoughts still come in every once in a while, but they don't last. I've learned to say STOP to them, turn them over to God, and think of something more pleasant. Sometimes I say STOP and then take 3 breaths. Other times I simply stay with the fear with all its sensations and watch as it fades away. Now I know I can deal with anything that comes my way, one breath at a time.

It is joyful to know that I can turn all my fears
over to God and breathe a sigh of relief.

"Mindfulness isn't about focused thinking,
introspection, self-analysis, or mindful gymnastics.
It's simply about bringing full attention—
not thinking—to whatever occurs."

—*Saki F. Santorelli*

As we sit and practice mindfulness, our minds might wander away hundreds of times. This is normal. Our minds are used to thinking. Meditation teacher Thich Nhat Hanh tells us that it is not important how many times our mind goes away from our breath, but how many times we bring it back.

This is the training of our minds:

back to the breath

over and over again.

Back to our breath

as we learn to be present

in

THIS

moment.

*Ahhh . . . the peace and joy to be found in THIS moment.
This is my practice today.*

"Because aging reminds us of our mortality,
it can be a primary stimulus to spiritual
awakening and growth."

—*Andrew Weil, M.D.*

While it is true that aging can be the touchstone for spiritual growth, it can also be the stimulus for depression. When we come to that time in our lives when we realize we are not going to live forever, it can be a crossroad pointing us in many different directions. Some of us make a conscious decision to lead a more spiritual life or continue the spiritual path we are on. We want to live a meaningful life, perhaps to return to our old religion or explore new spiritual directions.

Others might fall into depression, losing interest in activities that once gave us pleasure. We might find ourselves sitting in front of the TV more often or lost in the computer.

Yet others might follow that old slogan "Eat, drink and be merry for tomorrow you might die." We might pursue fast cars, gambling, or become addicted to alcohol or drugs, only to wonder at the end of the day why we are not really happy.

We are never too old or too young to explore what we think is important, to examine and reexamine how we want to live our lives.

*Today I am mindfully reexamining how I am living my life
and making sure I am on a spiritual path with a purpose.*

Go with the Flow

Today I will go with the flow,
    experiencing what is, and not trying to
    make it what I want it to be.
I will go with the flow, as they say,
    and at the end of the day
    I will bow my head
    and say thank you.

"As the turbulence of anxiety churns in the
subconscious and plays out in your thoughts and actions . . .
it can cause fatigue, sleep disorders, hormone imbalances,
health problems and premature aging."

—*Doc Childre and Deborah Rozman, Ph.D.*

Some anxiety is healthy. The feeling of flight or fight is encoded in our genes. It served our early ancestors when they were living in times of danger. It helps us today to know to jump out of the way from an oncoming car or when our lives are otherwise threatened. Adrenaline pours into our bloodstream, our heart rate increases, our breathing accelerates, and our blood vessels constrict.

Whether our anxiety is real or imagined doesn't matter. Our bodies react in the same way. Whether you imagine a lion is coming at you or a lion actually *is* coming at you, it creates the same reaction. When our stress is exaggerated it threatens our well-being.

Mindfulness can help us relax and deal with our anxieties in a healthy way. The more we make mindfulness a part of our lives, our anxieties decrease, our serenity increases, we become healthier, and our aging slows down.

*I am so glad that mindfulness is becoming more and
more a part of my life. The more I practice, the
calmer, happier, and more joyful I am.*

"Warm, eager, living life—to be rooted in life—
to learn, to desire to know, to feel, to think, to act.
That is what I want. And nothing less."

—Katherine Mansfield

*I aspire to be warm, eager, and affirming
every day of my life, no matter
how young or old I feel!*

goodbye stress hello joy

What we think is what we feel. Affirmations are wonderful techniques to use to change our minds from worry, fear, anxiety, anger, and other negative, stressful thoughts. Affirmations are simply positive statements. Affirmations have the power to change the chemicals in our brain and make our endorphins, our "feel good" chemicals, flow throughout our bodies. Simply stated, if we think angry thoughts our body feels tense. If we think peaceful thoughts we feel relaxed. Even if you feel fearful, you can turn that feeling around with an affirmation.

Affirmations have five parts to them to be successful. They have to be stated in the present moment. They must be positive. They must be possible. They must be personal. And we must state them with power and passion.

For example, if you are worried about getting a new job you can say: "God [or the universe, or Allah, or Spirit] is guiding me to the perfect job for me today." This opens you up to possibilities, rather than shutting you down with stress.

It feels so good to know I can change how I feel
in this moment by changing my thoughts!

"When we focus on only the external indications
of aging, we forget the internal treasures that we
accumulate with each year of our lives."

—Jean Smith

I t's true that we have less energy as we age. It's true that our body begins to change and there comes a time when we hardly recognize ourselves in the mirror.

It's also true that over the years we have learned many lessons and have accumulated at least some knowledge. Through all our experiences we hope we have gained some wisdom.

If we have been wise, we have grown spiritually, opening our hearts to love and compassion. As we mindfully continue on our spiritual path, our lives can grow richer and more fulfilling. We can grow closer to the God of our understanding.

*Today I am focusing on my internal
treasures, the positive qualities
I have accumulated over the years.*

time for reflections

"The root of the word 'question' is 'quest,'
and through the process of reflection, every question
becomes a quest, a journey of self-discovery."

—*Angeles Arrien*

I f we continue to make our lives a quest for meaning and purpose, no matter what our age, and live our life by our discov-
eries, joy will be our companion. No matter how busy we are,
taking time for quiet self-reflection brings us closer to God and
our true nature.

*Today I am finding great joy in taking time to sit quietly and
reflect on where I am now and where I am going.*

"This itself is the whole of the journey,
opening your heart to that
which is lovely."

—*The Buddha, from the Samyutta Nikaya*

I n a meditation class I led once, I asked the participants to hold up a hand mirror and say to themselves as they looked at their faces in the mirror:

"I am terrific just the way I am."

They did not like the way their faces looked in the mirror and made faces at themselves. I encouraged them to go beyond what they saw and look inside their hearts to see that they are good people full of compassion and love. Their intentions are to live a good life, to be honest and loving, and to help others when they can. I saw their faces soften when I said this and they smiled. Yes, age has changed our faces but it has also given many of us wisdom and a spiritual path to follow for a full, purposeful, and loving life. We need to look beyond the surface and value who we are and not what we look like.

I AM a terrific person just the way I am!

did you know?

"Neuroplasticity is our ability to change our mind,
to change ourselves and to change our perception of the
world around us: that is, our reality . . . we have to change
how the brain automatically and habitually works.
The ability to make our brain forgo its habitual internal
wiring and fire new patterns and combinations is
how neuroplasticity allows us to change."

—*Joe Dispenza, D.C.*

The good news is that our brains are *not* hardwired, as it has been thought until very recently. Scientists have now proven that we have the ability to rewire and create new neural circuits at any age! The other part of this exciting news is that our thoughts can rewire our brain. Mindfulness helps us to be aware of our thoughts and to distinguish them from healthy to unhealthy, joy-producing to stress-producing. The longer we practice mindfulness the more quickly we will be able to turn a negative thought into a positive one. The more we do this, we lessen our automatic reactions that produce stress and suffering and increase reactions that produce joy, compassion, love, and equanimity.

It is a joy to know that I can change my thoughts
and change my brain at any age and become
a happier, healthier person.

"The secret of meditation is to become conscious
of each moment of your existence."

—*Thich Nhat Hanh*

Mindfulness is a practice of quieting down our thoughts and being fully present in each moment. Meditation can be a time to quiet our mind, to simply notice what is going on in the present moment, a time to become balanced. It's a time when we connect with a deeper place in ourselves, with God, our soul, our inner spirit, the Buddha within, Allah, whatever you call a power greater than yourself. It is a spiritual practice. One can meditate and not be religious, and yet meditation is a part of most religions. Most important, it's a deeply personal experience.

Meditation teacher and author Christina Feldman tells us that "to undertake a period of meditation is to offer a gift to yourself." It is a time of exploring the most intimate relationship of your life—your relationship with yourself. Meditating weekly with a group is a very supportive and enriching experience. Finding a teacher you respect is most helpful. Develop a daily practice for which you make a commitment to take the time, no matter what else is going on in your life.

Mindfulness is a gift I give myself regularly, knowing how important it is for me spiritually. In meditation, I connect with a quiet place deep within me where I find peace and connect with my Higher Power.

"It's all about dreams. If I had to attribute
my success in life to any one thing it is this.
I believed in my dreams, even when
no one else did."

—*Oprah Winfrey*

No matter what age we are, we can still dream. There will always be something new to do, something different to enjoy, someone interesting to meet.

It does not matter that we do not have the energy of youth. We can dream about something that is reasonable for us, that is within our grasp, that fits who we are today, and it could be wonderful!

Today I am open to new ideas, new dreams, new adventures!

"A man can fail many times, but he isn't a failure
until he begins to blame somebody else."

—*John Burroughs*

We hear people all the time saying that their lives would be so much better if only "I had gotten that job," or "my mother wasn't an alcoholic," or "my father hadn't left us," or "I had gotten that scholarship to college."

Some people stay stuck their entire lives living in a resentment that things would be better if "_____." They hold on to the anger or their shame or their fixed ideas that they are stuck because of "_____."

When we learn to take responsibility for our own lives and not let our past dictate our future, then we can be free to be ourselves and live to our fullest potential. It's so important that we don't carry these destructive concepts with us as we grow older. We need to let go of everything that is holding us back, make peace with our past, and forgive our mistakes and the mistakes of those who we feel hurt us.

As mindfulness becomes more and more a part of us we can be more aware of the thoughts that have kept us stuck in our victim state and let them go. Only then can we be free to create the life we were meant to live.

I pray that I may be willing to let go of all my "if only's,"
all my regrets, and my blaming people, places, and things so
that I can live a rich life full of joy and peace and love.

23

My heart is filled
with
gratitude
for all
the
gifts
I have been given
in
my
life.

"The second half of a man's life is made up of nothing but the habits he has acquired during the first half."

—*Fyodor Dostoevsky*

I have difficulty eating breakfast early in the morning. In fact, after my inspirational reading, meditating, and maybe even writing while still in bed, I sometimes forget breakfast. If I go straight to my computer and begin writing, I might not think of eating until noon. I know this is not good for me. I know I will lose weight if I eat 3 meals a day, and yet this is how I flow. I am comfortable with this routine. But when I am serious about losing weight, I know I must change this routine. I know I must leave my comfort zone. And I know that it can take up to 21 days to change a habit. So I have to work on it. Sometimes it takes only a few days. Sometimes longer. But when it finally becomes a habit, it becomes my new comfort zone.

Over the years we accumulate many habits. Some are healthy, others are not. And the older we become, the more ingrained our habits are and they are harder to change.

It's good to take some time to be mindful of our habits every once in a while. Just notice them, without any judgments. Mindfulness helps us to observe our habitual actions and then make decisions as to whether or not they are healthy or detrimental mentally, physically, and spiritually. Make a decision to change. Just one thing at a time. You will be amazed how much better you will feel!

I pray for the guidance, patience, and willingness to begin to change one unhealthy habit, one day at a time.

"Sometimes, in the process of trying to
deny that things are always changing, we lose our
sense of the sacredness of life. We tend to forget that
we are part of the natural scheme of things."

—Pema Chödrön

Some days just feel more difficult as we age, and there is no law that says we have to push ourselves. Expectations about how we should feel can cause us great suffering.

Maybe we no long can play sports at the same intensity and skill we did when we were younger. Maybe we have to wear glasses and a hearing aid. Maybe the days we could be active for 16 hours become more like 12 hours or 10 hours or even 6 hours. The harder we try to be what we were, the more we suffer, and the more we disconnect from the sacredness of life. We are not in charge. There is a natural flow to the universe, and the more we can accept that we are part of it, the happier we will be. It's so much better to enjoy who we are in this moment, rather than trying to prove that we aren't aging and changing and able to do less.

*Today I am being mindful of my strengths
and limitations, letting myself appreciate my
life as it is, and that gives me great joy!*

good to know

"Neural plasticity is a revolutionary breakthrough with huge implications for people seeking better brain health and those looking to change stubborn patterns."

—*Kim Ward, Ph.D., and Hilary Stokes, Ph.D.*

We are filled with habits we have accumulated from the time we were born. Actually, some of our habits came even earlier, from our parents, grandparents, their parents, and so on. Some habits make us feel good, such as automatically saying thank you when someone does something nice for us or helping an older person. There are many habits that make us suffer, such as overspending or eating chocolate when we want to feel better.

Our mindful practice helps us recognize when we see a habit that is harmful to ourselves or others arise, or when we see one that makes us suffer over and over again. Rather than being upset with ourselves, beating ourselves up with guilt or embarrassment, we treat ourselves gently. Meditation teacher and author Thich Nhat Hanh suggests we simply smile. We replace the negative with a new and positive habit. By reacting in this new way we lessen the hold the old habit has on us and gradually our new habit becomes more and more automatic.

It is so good to know that I don't have to be stuck with my old, negative habits. I can breathe, smile, and change!

It feels so good to have a purpose today!

We're never too old to do something
useful for someone else.
We can always pick up the phone
and wish someone well,
or send loving thoughts and prayers
to someone in need.
It can be that simple,
that doable.
That helpful.

"Journal writing is a voyage to the interior."
—*Christina Baldwin*

It is so important to express how we feel, to release painful memories so we can freely move on with our lives. There are times we can write words we are incapable of saying aloud. Journaling can be a wonderful way to express these feeling and release them. I have frequently turned to my journal over the years as a vehicle to express what was going on in my life. Sometimes I've used it to record significant events, but most often I have journaled as a vehicle to help me through difficult times. At various times it has served as a bridge, allowing me to leave my pain behind so that I could move on; it has been a safe container for my feelings.

To express how we feel, whether to another person or to the pages of our journal, helps us along the path of healing. Let the words and feelings come out without concern for grammar or form, or even if your thoughts don't make any sense. Let your pages serve as a safe container for your thoughts and feelings. You never have to share these words with anyone. It is up to you.

I am willing to express all the feelings that have
been holding me back from living the joyous and authentic
life I was meant to live. I can search deep within me and
write them down in my journal, knowing every
step takes me to healing and freedom.

Should I or Shouldn't I?

Should I or Should I not . . .
Color my Hair?
Have a tummy tuck?
A face lift?
Get a wig?
Or just be me?

"To everything there is a season."

—*The Bible, Ecclesiastes*

I remember listening to my favorite singer when I was a teen-ager and hearing my father say, "You call this music? Why, in my day . . ." And he would go on and on.

While it certainly isn't true of all current music, I've surprised myself upon occasion by saying, "How can they like this? It's not even music, it's just noise!" And I never wanted to be a duplicate of my father!

Music styles change. Clothing styles change. Tastes change. The more we can let go of criticism and comparing and judging, the more we can go with the flow and the more comfortable we will feel as the world around us changes.

Today I will be more accepting of the changes I see around me. This will help me be a more content person.

There is a larger purpose
in the world
beyond my knowing.
Just to be a part of it is
a
blessing.

There is a wonderful legend about a man who was hoeing in his garden. One afternoon someone asked him to speculate on what he would do if he knew he was going to die that day. "I would hoe my garden," he replied. When I am faced with my death I would like to be so present to the task at hand that I would want to keep on with whatever happened to be my particular hoeing.

Wouldn't it be wonderful if we could live each day like this, being awake and alive to exactly what we are doing?

Today I am being present to each moment,
treasuring the moment
I am in with joy.

"If we truly mourn the losses of old age,
mourning can liberate us, can lead us to a creative
freedom, further development, joy and
the ability to embrace life."

—*Judith Viorst*

I t's impossible to deny our aging process. We just need to look in the mirror! We just need to get up in the morning and feel more aches and pains and less energy. It's impossible to deny that parts of our body begin to age and we visit our doctors more frequently.

How can we actually mourn these changes, these losses, so we can move beyond them to a rich life?

We need to be mindful and honest. If we're angry, express it! If we're sad, feel it! Even if we are depressed, allow ourselves to feel it. Denying or burying any of our feelings just prolongs our unhappiness. It keeps us from moving forward and enjoying the life we have.

Today I am mindful of all my feelings,
free to be exactly where I am and
who I am in each moment.

with the help of mindfulness

*I can wake up each morning with
the intention not to do harm.*

*I am so grateful that I never stop
learning and that I can continue to grow as a
compassionate and loving human being.*

"The real voyage of discovery consists not in seeking
new landscapes, but in having new eyes."

—*Marcel Proust*

Last year my life changed. My breath grew short. When I exerted myself, pains shot through my heart. My throat often constricted, and I could not swallow. My doctor ordered test after test—lungs, heart, blood, CT scan. First she prescribed antibiotics, then three asthma medicines, then GERD medicine, then antidepressants. Finally, after I lost 20 pounds, panicked daily, and became convinced I would die if I kept losing weight, another doctor diagnosed gall bladder disease.

Today, 12 months later, I am free of anxiety, depression, and medicines. I am mostly peaceful. How? I meditate every day. And as part of my meditation, I remember that my body is of a nature to get sick, but it is also of a nature to heal. I remember that my body is of a nature to age and die, but I am one with God.

I used to be terrified of loss, aging, sickness, and death. Now, by practicing remembering that they are part of life, I am not scared by them anymore. They just are. And through some mysterious alchemy, my acceptance of loss, aging, sickness, and death helps me to cherish the beauty of life even more.

—*Susan Walsh*

*I have turned all my fears over to God
and I am free and at peace.*

FEBRUARY

> "Our lives do not have to be limited
> by our past experiences."
>
> —*Rosalyn Carter*

Just because we may not be able to play a good competitive game of tennis anymore or we find that mountain climbing is too difficult, it does not mean that we aren't able to move forward into new ventures. Perhaps we tried ballet before and found we weren't good at it. Now we might find ballroom dancing fun.

Maybe we aspired to be a Major League baseball player and couldn't even make the college team. Playing softball with people our age might bring us a lot of joy.

Look inside and do some soul searching. Listen to your intuition. Wait for an inner stirring. What's calling you? What are you moved to do?

Give it a try. If not the first thing that comes, maybe the second or third. There are many activities out there just waiting to be discovered!

> *Today I am letting God guide me to where the*
> *fun is and I am putting aside all*
> *fears of failure and doubt.*

> "Today, women in their 60s and
> over celebrate life!"
>
> *—Cher*

I have a special memory of my grandmother when she was 62 and I was just two and a half. I lived in Detroit at the time and we flew to New York to visit her because she was sick. We found her sitting in a chair, soaking her feet in a pail of soapy water, and she looked so old. Of course, I was very young then so anything over 20 years old probably looked very old to me, but older people did dress very different from young people back then. My mother always wore a dress until she was in her late 60s and I found it hard to get used to her in slacks. Twenty-five years later, when my kids were growing up, I was wearing jeans, sneakers, and sweatshirts just like them.

Back in the '50s many thought it inappropriate for baseball star Ted Williams not to wear a tie at special events. Today no one thinks twice about such a thing because people dress in a variety of styles and almost anything goes.

*It feels so good that I have let go of meaningless,
rigid rules about how I should look and am more
relaxed about how I appear to others.*

Breathing in I'm aware of my breathing
Breathing out I'm aware of my breathing
Breathing in I'm aware of my breath entering my body
Breathing out I'm aware of my breath leaving my body
Breathing in I'm aware of my body just as it is . . .
All of it, with all the changes that have
come as I have been growing older.

In spite of some of the aches and pains,
I'm filled with compassion for all my body can do.
I'm filled with gratitude.
I'm filled with joy.

"Worry never robs tomorrow of its sorrow,
it only saps today of its joy."

—Leo Buscaglia

What do we worry about as we grow older? Losing our sight? Our hearing? Our memories, of course! We might worry about losing our money, our homes, or our partners. But scary for many of us is our ability to take care of ourselves, our ability to be independent, to drive. So much to lose! And yes, some of this will happen to some of us unless we die painlessly in our sleep before we experience any losses.

Of course we know that worrying about any of these losses will not change anything and will only create greater suffering in our lives. They will either happen or not.

So what can we do so that we don't worry and are able to find joy as we grow older? Stay in the moment. Be mindful in each moment. Enjoy each moment, and most important, be grateful in each moment for what we have.

*Today I am filling my heart as I do
everything in my life for which I am grateful,
and I smile at how very lucky I am.*

41

with the help of mindfulness

I can look deeply into my pain and find its origin.
Only then can I be free to move forward.

"I have arrived, I am home, in the
here and in the now."
—*from* A Basket of Plums *songbook*

This present moment contains my whole life, all of it: the pain, happiness, mistakes, harm done, joys, loves, and triumphs. In my precious life is all of human history, its past and future. In my body, spirit, and mind, I am interconnected to all that is, to Mother Earth, to my parents, my son and his child, and all future generations. I am connected to all suffering people on earth and to all the sources of joy and freedom that have ever existed or will exist. I am enormous. I feel as large as the Pacific Ocean, as deep, as full of life, and as free to feel the sun over my entire surface. I have arrived. I am home, in this body, in this spirit, in the here and in the now. I like seeing my face in the mirror just as I am, the age I am today. I am free. I am free. I am free.

—*Joann Malone*

Sit quietly in mindfulness . . .

> Wait.
>
> Listen to the stirrings of your inner spirit.
>
> Open to the message.
>
> What is it telling you to do?
>
> Where is it telling you to go?
>
> Trust your inner voice.
>
> Don't let the "I'm too old" voice hold you back.

"You're only as old as you feel."

—*Popular saying*

There are times when our physical conditions make us feel much older than our chronological age. It can be easy to slip into self-pity or negative thinking, forgetting that the more we dwell on our pain or disabilities, the more pain we feel. Whatever we feel in our bodies we do not need to make worse by thinking about it in our minds or feeling it with our emotions. We need to remember we are not our pain.

*I feel so much lighter when I accept what is
going on with my body and do not add
to the pain with stressful thinking.*

As I begin this day with prayer and meditation,
I let go of all the regrets from the past
and all my fears of the future.
I feel love in this moment.
I am at peace.
My heart is filled with gratitude.

"Beautiful young people are accidents of nature,
but beautiful old people are works of art."

—*Eleanor Roosevelt*

As we age we do begin to lose our strength physically, but we can still grow stronger spiritually. Morning inspirational readings of sages and wise elders help us to set our spiritual intention for the day. We put less value on having things and more value in our relationships to our family, friends, and our planet.

We can stretch our hearts and fill them with more compassion and love. We can be mentors to those younger than us, serve in food banks, or read to the blind, for example.

Looking deeply within with prayer and meditation, we can ask ourselves, *What can I do to help someone else?*

> *Today, in prayer and meditation, I ask*
> *for the guidance and strength to live my life*
> *with more devotion to serving others.*

> "As long as I am grasping for the mind
> I had 20 years ago, I suffer."
>
> —*Susan Moon*

My mother used to make notes to herself and put them everywhere. In the evening she would write a to-do list and put it at the front door. She would take it to work with her in the morning so she would remember what to buy before coming home.

Before having company she would have lists everywhere. When she set the table she would put out her serving dishes and have a little piece of paper on each one: bread, chopped liver, sweet potato casserole, and so on.

At the time I didn't realize it but now I see that she was the epitome of acceptance. She had given up any struggle, any attempt to remember what needed to be done and where things needed to be placed. She had total acceptance in the state of her memory so she was open to going about her preparations and then to enjoying her company.

I keep forgetting to drink 8 glasses of water, which will help my leg cramps. I forget to do my neck, back, and posture exercises. I forget to get up every hour for my oh-so-sore body as I hunch over my computer for hours at a time.

I need to borrow a page from my mother and begin to leave notes everywhere. If only I could remember where I put them!

I pray to learn how to make my life easier
by adjusting to my limitations.

"Today I am stopping to take the time
to do all I can do to help trigger my memory.
It makes my life so much easier! We carry within
us the wonders we seek without us."

—*Thomas Brown*

Our gifts lie patiently within us, waiting to be discovered while we go about our busy lives. Now we can take the time to find them, one by one, by clearing out our blocks to them, one by one.

Aging can bring us the gift of slowing down so we can look deeply. With less physical energy, the constant busyness is no longer our companion. If we let ourselves experience time in silence and meditation, we can truly find the gift of ourselves.

No matter how busy I think I am today,
I am making mindfulness a part of my day.
I am taking the time to look within and getting in
touch with the specialness of who I am.

I can look back with regret;
I can look forward with fear;
or
I can choose
to be
in this
one precious moment
with this
one precious breath
knowing I have
everything
I
need
in this moment
and
it
is
perfect.

"Love heals, Love renews.
Love makes you feel safe.
Love brings you closer to God.
Love conquers all fear.
Love makes you young.
Love reverses the aging process."

—*Deepak Chopra*

Today is a wonderful day to connect with someone you love. It can be your partner or children or friends. It's a day to fill your heart with love. And if you cannot make a physical connection, you can write, email, Skype, or call.

Let this day be about love.

Today my heart is filled with love as I think
about all the special people in my life.

"Tell me what you feel in your room when
the full moon is shining upon you and your lamp is
dying out, and I will tell you how old you are,
and I shall know if you are happy."

—*Henri Frederic Arniel*

We hear so much today that it is not what we have that makes us happy but who we are inside and what we do with our lives. The poets and the philosophers tell us about the joy of each day, and many times we agree and then go on with life as usual. Many of us still think that if we had more money for retirement or a better car or a better home, or a more loving partner, we would be happy. If we only had something, just something, that we don't have, we would be happier!

Hopefully, as we grow older, we learn that it really isn't the things outside us that give us joy. It really is who we are inside.

We can have so much!

The joy of nature, and good friends and those we love.

What we feel in our hearts when we are

grateful and generous and compassionate and forgiving.

When we help another person or hold a baby or a puppy.

Is there really anything else we truly need that will make us happier?

*I am so grateful for the gift of my life and all the possibilities
that I can experience which bring me deep and lasting joy.*

"If you suffer, it is not because things are impermanent.
It is because you believe things are permanent."

—*Thich Nhat Hanh*

As we age, losses are more common than uncommon. We lose partners, jobs, and dear friends. Some of us even experience the painful tragedy of losing children. Some lose status, retirement savings. Friends and family move away for good. Flowers fade. Trees lose their leaves. Ponds dry up. If we're lucky, we have gained some wisdom. We become more spiritual. Some of us make a deeper connection to God, to a higher purpose. We come to see that we are a part of an ever-changing cycle of birth and death, an ebb and flow. We come to trust our place in the universe and choose to be grateful for this day—today—for this moment now.

Today I am filled with gratitude for this breath,
this moment, this life, this opportunity, whatever is in
front of me—right now. I am so grateful for
the gift of my time on this earth.

"Water says to the one who has gotten dirty: Come!
The dirty one answers: But I'm so ashamed . . .
Water answers: But how will you
get clean without me?"

—*Rumi*

Rumi's quote will have different meanings for everyone. Why not make this your practice today? Are you still carrying shame? Are you still afraid to be seen exactly as you are, the you that you have hidden and the you that you show to the world?

To whom are you afraid to show your true self? Are you willing to completely accept yourself, just as you are today, knowing that no one is perfect and that you will never be perfect?

It is so freeing to accept myself completely,
without shame and with love and compassion for all of me,
exactly as I am. I pray that I may have the willingness
to move toward complete acceptance.

"Gratitude unlocks the fullness of life.
It turns what we have into enough, and more.
It turns denial into acceptance, chaos to order,
confusion to clarity. It can turn a meal into a feast,
a house into a home, a stranger into a friend.
Gratitude makes sense of our past, brings peace
for today, and creates a vision for tomorrow."

—*Melody Beattie*

What a wonderful time we are all living in! We have evolved to the point where many things are available to us. We can have hip and knee replacements, heart and liver transplants, surgeries that can remove tumors and surgeries that replace limbs. We can wear glasses to improve our fading sight and hearing aids that improve the fading sounds. And we have pills that ease our physical suffering, lift our depressions, and lower our cholesterol, just to name a few.

*I feel myself softening and filling with joy and
I live with more gratitude in my life.*

good news

In studies inspired by the Dalai Lama, it has been discovered that the brain and its functions are adaptable to change and that mindfulness can increase the brain's power of attention to respond with flexibility to stressful events.

It has also been found in other studies that stress ages our bodies and our brains more quickly. It actually thins the grey matter of our brain!

*It feels so good to know that my mindfulness
practice helps me to deal better with stress
and to slow down my aging process.*

"Work as though you're going to live forever.
Live as though you're going
to die tomorrow."

—Edith White, my mother-in-law,
quoting a Russian proverb

I love getting older! True, my body parts—bones, muscles, joints, brain, and everything else, not all of them pleasant to mention—are not working as well as they used to, and I worry occasionally about what life will be like if any parts fail me completely before I die. But I understand life so much better now, and I appreciate it so much more! I know that pain, loss, misunderstandings, and clashes of personality are inevitable, and that I can learn to live with them and soften around them; I realize that the things people say and do reveal how they are in their lives, right now, and are not so much about me; and I respect my elders more than I ever did when I was young!

Today I am living as though this day is my last,
deciding what is important to do, and
what is important to overlook.

—Samantha M. White

"Mindfulness is simply being aware of what
is happening right now without wishing it were different;
enjoying the pleasant without holding on when it changes
(which it will); being with the unpleasant without fearing
it will always be this way (which it won't)."

—*James Baraz*

It is obvious that as we grow older, we can no longer do the things we once did. Our bodies lose strength and flexibility. Aches and pains are more frequent. Depending on how well we cared for our bodies, our ability to play many sports diminishes. Our hair turns white or gray or even falls out or thins. But the mind . . . ahhh, the mind. Here is where the greatest lessons lie. The impermanence of our memory. Where did I put the car keys? Why did I just walk into this room? Why did I put the shampoo in the refrigerator? How did I forget that doctor's appointment?

These are often called "senior moments." It can be a most frustrating and embarrassing time of our lives. Or, we can practice mindfulness. While this practice does not guarantee that our memory will be as it was, it has been proven that it can keep us sharper and more alert.

*What a blessing it is to live in an age where we know
that our brain can continue to grow when we are mindful.
I am so grateful for this knowledge and this practice.*

goodbye stress
hello joy

One way of using mindfulness to bring greater joy into your life as you age is with visualizations. First, sit with your breath and let yourself quiet down. When you feel relaxed, let yourself imagine where your heart is in your body and breathe into this area. Quietly breathe in and breathe out, letting your breath be natural. No need to breathe deeper. No need to change your breath at all. Then imagine something that brings joy into your life.

Perhaps it is holding a newborn baby or a puppy. Perhaps it is spending time with nature, in the woods, mountains, or near the ocean. Maybe it's eating chocolate! Whatever it is, imagine yourself doing this for a few minutes. Now smile while you see yourself in this activity. This is a wonderful exercise for the times when you can't actually take part in a favorite activity.

"When we realize that illness is inescapable,
that stress around illness increases our suffering,
and that being sick is not a shortcoming—
only then can we be at ease with, and
even empowered by, our illness."

—*Author Unknown*

*Today I am accepting with mindfulness exactly
what is going on in my body. I am letting
go and letting God help me to trust
the natural process of life.*

"I prefer to call mindfulness a way of being. . . .
It's rather that you can bring awareness to any state you
happen to be in. There's nothing wrong with being caught
up in difficult, stressful, agitated, or confusing moments."

—*Jon Kabat-Zinn*

It is said that a farmer once came to see the Buddha in order
to seek advice. The farmer had many problems and he told the
Buddha, in great detail, all about how they made his life very
difficult. He went on and on about the weather, his wife, his children, neighbors, and more.

The Buddha replied simply, "I cannot help you get rid of those
problems."

The man, now exasperated, asked the Buddha, "What kind
of teacher are you? And if you are so enlightened, what can you
help me get rid of?" The Buddha replied, "I can help you get rid
of your 84th problem." "And what is my 84th problem?" "Your
84th problem is that you assume your life will be better if you get
rid of your other 83 problems."

*Today I know that everything I can do,
including prayer and meditation, will never take
away all my problems or bring me happiness.
I can have problems and, by accepting them,
come to a place of balance, contentment,
and even joy.*

time for reflections

"There is a fountain of youth:
it is your mind, your talents, the creativity
you bring to your life and the lives of the
people you love. When you learn to tap this
source, you will have truly defeated age."

—*Sophia Loren*

Today I am choosing to think about the positive aspects of aging. What have I learned? What do I have to pass on to others?

*Today I am taking time by myself in mindful reflection
on the qualities I have that make my life
richer as I grow older.*

"Mindfulness is the aware, balanced
acceptance of the present experience.
It isn't more complicated than that. It is opening
to or receiving the present moment, pleasant
or unpleasant, just as it is, without either
clinging to it or rejecting it."

—*Sylvia Boorstein*

The practice of mindfulness can bring us many gifts as we age. It can help us uncover our false premises, assumptions, conclusions, and beliefs, thus opening our minds to the truth.

It can open our hearts to love, compassion, and forgiveness, thus giving us the freedom to be with everyone, just as they are.

It can help us accept our strengths and our weaknesses, our flaws and our imperfections, thus allowing us to give up our shame of not being good enough.

Mindfulness can teach us how to be real . . . in this moment.

*Today I am letting my life flow as I find joy and
acceptance in being me, exactly as I am.*

my practice

Mindful Listening

"... Mountains and hills shall break out in song before you,
And all the trees of the countryside shall clap their hands."

—*Isaiah, 55:12*

It is wonderful to take time to listen, to stop and hear the birds singing or the waves crashing, the barely audible sound of a grasshopper jumping, or the rustle of leaves being lifted by the breeze. If you can, take a walk and listen to the sounds of nature. Walk in a field of wild flowers or along the shore. Climb up a mountain or down into a valley. You can picture scenes like this when listening to Julie Andrews singing with such joy the immortal lyrics: "The hills are alive with the sound of music."

If you can't get outside, open your window and listen to see if you can hear birds amidst the sound of traffic, perhaps a dog barking, or leaves rustling, or a bumblebee flying by. And if it's too cold to open your window, simply listen to the sounds of your breath going in and going out as you meditate. Stopping to listen is a meditation in itself. It's a way of slowing ourselves down, going deeper inside ourselves and finding that special place where wisdom sometimes hides.

Today I am finding great joy in taking the time to stop and listen, connecting to all that is perfect each moment.

I am taking all the time I need to take care of myself today, to be gentle with myself, to listen deeply to my inner being, my wise self, and to flow gently with what I hear.

Thoughts actually produce a biochemical reaction in our brain. If we think a pleasant thought we feel pleasant and if we react to something and think angry thoughts we obviously feel unhappy.

We often react automatically to people and situations. Perhaps we respond with anger when we feel hurt. Or we might slip into self-pity when we are put down or left out. Our thoughts start on their own, as if a CD is playing over and over and we keep repeating our reactions automatically.

The following is a very simple exercise we can do to change our habits. The more we practice it, the more our brain will get used to the shift and we will begin to feel what is going on now in a more healthy and appropriate way.

The next time you feel yourself reacting emotionally to something that is said to you, or something you are experiencing:

> Think STOP
> Think RELEASE with your out breath
> Then SMILE with your in breath
> and SMILE with your out breath
> > *feeeel* the peace!

MARCH

"Don't run away. It's that simple."

—*Jack Kornfield*

Over the years we have developed many means by which we try to avoid emotional pain. Some of us have used alcohol or drugs. Other shop, gamble, eat, work, watch TV, or even exercise. But all we have accomplished is to push our pain deep inside, and it has served as a block to joy. Block pain, block joy. It's that simple. Once we block pain we close our heart to feeling all emotions, including joy, love, and compassion.

Years ago when I was applying for a mortgage I didn't really know if we could pay for it. Full of fear, I found myself close to a panic attack. I was new at mindfulness and decided to try what I had been learning. I pulled my car over into a parking lot and simply let the feelings flow over me. I must have sat there for at least fifteen minutes, being aware of my heart pounding, and actually sweating. Soon those sensations began to subside. My fists unclenched. My breathing was more regular. I knew then I could handle any feeling, pleasant or unpleasant, and be all right.

Facing life in each moment certainly does not always feel comfortable, but it is the only way we can be free to really be alive. Mindfulness can help us to be with our emotions but not hold on to them. By having them we can release them.

Today I am practicing being here in each moment.
I am feeling everything. It feels so good to be alive!

I can look back with regret.
I can look forward with fear.
Or,
I can choose
to be
in this
one precious moment
with this
one precious breath
knowing I have
everything
    I
      need
        in this moment
          and
            it
              is
                perfect.

my practice

Mindful Eating

Mindful eating is a wonderful way to develop the habit of being in the present moment. It helps us to slow down, reflect, and see how connected we are. You can imagine all the people it took to bring the variety of food to your table. There are those who prepare the soil, plant the seeds, harvest the plants, transport the food to be processed and packed. Then those who transport it to the store and the people who unpack the boxes.

Here is a wonderful prayer written by meditation teacher and author Thich Nhat Hanh. It is nice to recite this before eating.

The Five Contemplations

This food is the gift of the whole universe, the earth, the sky, and much hard work.

May we eat in mindfulness so that we may be worthy of receiving it.

May we transform our unskillful states of mind and learn to eat with moderation.

May we take only foods that nourish us and prevent illness.

We accept this food so that we may realize the path of understanding and love.

We accept this food so that we may nurture our sisterhood and brotherhood, strengthen our community, and nourish our ideal of serving all beings.

"The more I work with people and the
more I go through life, the more I realize that
people just want to be happy. If I take five minutes
out of each day to remember to treat people
the same way I want to be treated, we can
accomplish wonderful things together."

—*Bob Fishel*

My son was a very wise young man when he wrote this at around 25 years old. He had discovered a basic truth about happiness. We all want to be happy. When we find out what makes us truly happy, we can pass that along to others. Compassion, love, forgiveness, and generosity are just a few things that make us happy and it is wonderful to discover that when we give this to others, we still have it. Another beautiful truth is that the more we give away, the more we have.

Today I am reaching deep into my heart and
sharing my goodness with others.

Breathing in to all the
aches and pains in my body
I am releasing
my
tension
Breathing in to all the
aches and pains in my body
I am softening
my pain
Breathing in
Breathing out
I am feeling better

"Your body is precious. It is our vehicle
for awakening. Treat it with care."

—*The Buddha*

When we were younger we could go, go, go, from dawn 'til midnight, doing anything and everything we wanted to do. Gradually that changed. Perhaps we found ourselves going to bed a bit earlier, or even taking an occasional nap. We realized we couldn't do as much as we had previously and we found this upsetting. Acceptance! It's the key to peace of mind and joy. Just as we have learned to budget our money, we have to do the same with our time and energy. Look at your day before you and decide what is most important. Then decide what is realistic. The day will be far more enjoyable!

Today I know it is okay to do less.
It's all a part of taking loving care of myself.

"If older women didn't mind looking old,
a huge section of the economy would collapse.
There are so many companies that sell millions
of dollars to help us look better as we age!"

—*Susan Moon*

I have been using the same brand of face cream for years because my mother used it and she looked great in her 70s! The company has now come out with many new anti-aging, antiwrinkle creams. They now have antiwrinkle cream for your face, your eyes, and even your body. And the price goes up with each new product. And these products are not just for women either. Clever ads about men trying to look younger for a new job and a pretty young gal now are on television and in the papers.

I'm fortunate. I have my mother's and father's genes that also produce very little gray hair well into my 70s. I joke about dyeing my hair gray because my hair doesn't match my face.

While dyeing one's hair and having face-lifts and body tucks doesn't actually fit into the realm of acceptance of ourselves as we are, they make people feel better. And I don't think there is anything wrong with doing what makes you feel better as long as it isn't at the expense of anyone else.

It's good to live in an age which gives me
so many choices about how I look!

*I am accepting with mindfulness
exactly what is going on in my body.
I am letting go and letting God help me to
trust the natural process of life.*

If it didn't matter
what anyone else thought
about what I should do . . .
what would I do?

"Worry is a thin stream of fear trickling through the mind.
If encouraged, it cuts a channel into which
all other thoughts are drained."

—*Author unknown*

Worry is not problem solving. Worry is not looking for a solution. We know worry doesn't help anything to improve. We know worry drains us and creates stress in our lives. We know worry leads to many forms of illness. And worry ages us! So why do so many of us worry? Because that's typical of human nature.

One person told me, "Of course I worry! I love my children! I wouldn't be a good mother if I didn't worry." She thinks she's accomplishing something, although she isn't.

Worry is fear-based. We worry we are not going to get what we want when we want it. We worry we are not good enough. We worry if it is going to rain on our picnic. And all this gets us nowhere.

Instead of going over and over the same problem, why not ask yourself if there is something you can do about it? If so, do it! If not, let go.

Bring your awareness to your breath and breathe in and out three times. Let yourself relax. You will be much freer to find a solution, if there is one, when you are not filled with stress; and, if there isn't one, pray for acceptance. This isn't easy if you have been a worrier all your life, but it is important if you want to be healthy as you age.

It feels so good to turn my problems over to the
care of God, do what I can, and let go.

The Five Remembrances

"I am of the nature to grow old. There is no way to escape
   growing old.
I am of the nature to have ill health. There is no way to escape
   having ill health.
I am of the nature to die. There is no way to escape death.
All that is dear to me and everyone I love are of the nature to
   change. There is no way to escape being separate from them.
I inherit the results of my actions of body, speech, and mind.
   My actions are my continuation."

—The Buddha

The five remembrances help us identify and look deeply at our fears. At first they may sound very depressing. They did to me! After all, who wants to even think about these situations? I found that after reading them for a few days, I became more comfortable with them. I began to accept that they are a part of life that needs to be faced eventually. Why not now? And the more I read them, they became a part of my life.

Yes, I am of the nature to grow old, and so forth. But I am also of the nature to grow in love and compassion and to live a full and rich life. I am also of the nature to have joy in my life!

*Today I am accepting life on life's terms
and that is so freeing!*

"We have a lamp inside of us, the lamp of
mindfulness, which we can light anytime. The oil of that
lamp is our breathing, our steps, and our peaceful smile.
We have to light up that lamp of mindfulness so
that light will shine out and the darkness will dissipate
and cease. Our practice is to light up the lamp."

—*Thich Nhat Hanh*

The older we are, the more time we have had to accumulate how we respond to our world. Our habitual thoughts and reactions are as much a part of us as our taste in clothing, food, or music. Mindfulness gives us the opportunity to observe whether these mental habits create happiness or suffering for us.

For example, I saw that as soon as someone tells me what to do I react. I instantly think, "Leave me alone! I know what I am doing!" I feel the anger rise in me and the tension in my body. When I shared this with Joanne Friday, one of my teachers, she suggested I look deeply and find earlier times when I felt the same way. Then I should give this younger me lots of love and hugs.

First I saw my ex-husband telling me how to rake leaves and I remember the same feelings and thinking, "Why doesn't he leave me alone? I'm doing just fine." Looking deeper, I found numerous times my father told me his way was better. I became stubborn and angry when someone told me what to do. With mindfulness I have learned to breathe into that feeling, relax, and decide whether or not I want to accept suggestions.

*With the help of mindfulness I can change
my automatic thoughts and reactions. It feels so good
to know I am not too old to change.*

time for reflections

This evening, when I look back upon my day,
will it be one in which I can take pride?
Can I be mindful of my speech and my actions
so I have no regrets?
Or will there be amends I need to make
to myself and others?
Will I feel joy or will I feel regret?
And if I do feel regrets
about mistakes I have made,
can I forgive myself
and let go
so I can feel joy?

*I pray that I may live this day mindfully, with
love, compassion, and acceptance.*

"It's not how old you are but
how you are old."

—*Jules Renard*

I am presently in the fourth quarter of my life. Young people might laugh, but I still consider myself a work in progress.

While I do have fixed ideas, they have come about through experience. However, I am able to be open to new ideas, I can laugh at myself, and I can find absurdity in my behavior and in that of others.

I know that joy is sometimes fleeting, but it still comes to me and embraces me warmly and I am grateful.

—*Sandy Bierig*

*Today I am open to fun
and funny events.*

"No matter how well we are prepared,
the moment belongs to God."

—*Sheldon Knoff*

Most of us, at one time or other, will have to make serious decisions in our lives. Perhaps we will have to or want to downsize. What to take? What to give away? What to sell? Where to go? Am I close to having to live with my children? Do I have enough money to go into assisted living? What if I need a nursing home? We might be faced with these and many other questions. Perhaps we will choose to be independent until we actually can't anymore. One of the hardest decisions for many will be, *When do I have to stop driving?*

Depressing as some of these questions might be, they do have to be addressed. The best we can do is plan, save, and then take life as it comes, trusting we will know what to do and when to do it when the time comes.

*It feels so good to know that no matter
how well I do prepare, God is always here.
God is ultimately in charge and
always on time.*

"To a happy person, the formula for happiness
is quite simple: Regardless of what happened early this
morning, last week, or last year—or what may happen
later this evening, tomorrow, or three years from
now—now is where happiness lies."

—*Richard Carlson*

There's a wonderful story that illustrates how we carry the past into our present moment, whether or not it is appropriate.

A mother was teaching her daughter how to cook pot roast and explained to her that she should cut off the end before putting it in a pan. The daughter asked why and her mother said, "I don't know. That's how my mother cooked pot roast." The daughter was curious and went to her grandmother with the same question. "I don't know," answered her grandmother. "That's how my mother cooked pot roast." Still curious, the daughter went to her great-grandmother, who answered, "The pot was too small."

So if we are doing things the way we have always done them, if we are acting and reacting from habit and automatic reactions, if we are carrying fears around aging that have been passed down to us by society, how can we change? How can we be fresh and new in each moment?

We can learn to practice mindfulness and that feels so good!

"How wonderful it is that nobody need wait
a single moment before starting
to improve the world."

—*Anne Frank*

I stopped smoking over 28 years ago. Before that I was a very heavy smoker, and for many of those years I would drop my finished cigarette to the ground, crush it with my foot, and leave it there. When I first met my partner I saw her crush out her cigarette the same way but then lean over, pick it up, and put it in her pocket, so that later she could throw it away. Until that moment, I must admit, I had no awareness that I was cluttering the earth. I did what I always did, what I had seen others do since I began smoking and gave it no thought. As soon as I became conscious of my inconsideration, my lack of thoughtfulness, I never did it again.

If we are mindful as we become older, we become more and more conscious of the things we do and don't do that contribute to the happiness or suffering of others. We discover ways that we can make life better. The more mindful we are, the more we can improve our life and our environment.

*It feels so good to know I can make a difference
in my own world and the world around
me with my actions.*

I feel at peace today
knowing that I am being led
by a power greater than myself.
I am exactly where I need to be
in this time
of my life.

"When something intolerable is in my life, I head for the
water. It leavens me in some way. Some middle-most part
of me is soothed and silenced by it."

—*Alice Koller*

People are drawn to nature for healing. We can find solace walking along the beach, gliding in a canoe on a clear pond, hiking in the woods, weeding our garden, or taking a walk in the park.

Some therapists believe that deepening our emotional ties to nature is as vital to our well-being as the close personal bonds we pursue with family and friends. In his book *The Celestine Prophecy,* James Redfield wrote: "When you appreciate the beauty and uniqueness of things, you receive energy."

One of the things I heard, after my son died, was that there was healing in hugging a tree. I had no idea whether or not there was any truth in this, but I was willing to try anything. The idea is that everything is full of energy and that trees are something substantial that we can feel with our entire bodies. They are alive and growing and very powerful. When I was sure no one was looking, I found a large tree and put my arms around it. Holding myself close to the trunk, it actually felt good.

We can take breaks during the day or night to connect with nature by spending a few moments looking out the window, watching the clouds, sky, moon, or stars. If an outside view isn't available, we can create our own indoor garden with potted plants. Simply being mindful in nature reduces our stress and keeps our mind, body, and spirits healthy.

I feel powerful healing energy when I connect with nature.
I am making sure I take the time to make this a regular part of my day.

Every blade of grass has its angel that
bends over it and whispers,
"Grow, grow."

—*The Talmud*

*Today I am smiling with joy as I follow
God's will for me, growing mentally,
physically, and spiritually.*

"Joy is what happens to us when we allow ourselves
to recognize how good things really are."

—*Marianne Williamson*

It feels so good that I have come to the place in my life where I can say that I am a satisfied woman. I made a list about the joys of turning 65 that included some of the areas of my life in which I am no longer searching for "more." I have enough of everything I really need. I have all the material possessions and relationships that are most important in my life. I no longer need to search for a bigger, better anything—house, husband, family, town, career, community, sangha, or spiritual path. This doesn't mean that there will be no changes in any of those areas. There will be inevitably. But I'm not *seeking* changes. I'm no longer *looking* for a different mate, house, career, community, God. This realization brings me great peace and joy.

—*Joann Malone*

*I am so grateful I can accept what
is in my life with joy!*

time for reflections

There's always a lot to be thankful for
if you take time to look for it. For example,
I am sitting here thinking how nice
it is that wrinkles don't hurt.

—Author unknown

What other aspects of aging can you turn around from negative to positive?

*Today I am choosing to think about
the positive aspects of aging.*

89

my practice

As a young child, I feared death.
As a youth, I feared life.
As a man, I made life a struggle.
Now I've lost my fear of death and life.
When I die, I'll go home, that's all. Until then,
I treat every day as a precious gift, every moment as a wonder.
As I age I appreciate more and more the rare gift of life,
the beauty and wondrous variety of this world, and the courage and creativity of all those beings who have come before me,
upon whose shoulders I stand.
As I age I have less anxiety, and more fun,
fewer doubts, and more confidence.
less ego, and more love.
I have come home to the marvelous present.

—*Andrew Rock*

Imagine new neural pathways forming in your brain as you
    think positive thoughts.

Imagine new neural pathways forming in your brain as you try
    something new.

Imagine the happiness part of your brain getting larger as you
    practice mindfulness.

Imagine your heart opening as your willingness to forgive
    someone expands.

And feel the joy as your capacity for generosity grows in you . . .
    one day at a time.

> "Physical pain is unavoidable but meditation
> practice can ease the mental suffering
> that often accompanies it."
>
> —*Susan Smalley and Diana Winston*

There's no avoiding some aches and pains as we grow older. We can do many things to lessen them, such as yoga, stretching, exercise, and meditation, but we will still have some pain.

Dr. Susan Bauer-Wu's work focuses on the clinical application of meditation and its effects on health and the quality of life in individuals with serious illness, especially cancer. She teaches that it's not the pain that brings us suffering but how we react to it.

Be mindful of the stories that you repeat in your head and to anyone who will listen to you. Be mindful when you begin to list over and over again what is wrong with you, thus continuing to bring your pain to the forefront of your mind. Be mindful about noticing whether you think about your pain often.

Accept and don't resist. Resistance tightens up our muscles and intensifies the pain. Relaxation helps to release the pain. Allow the pain to be there. Meditation helps us to relax and breathe into our pain. Mindfulness helps us be aware of our thoughts and let them go.

> *I am so grateful that my mindfulness practice*
> *helps me deal better with the aches and pains*
> *that are a natural part of aging.*

"God grant me the serenity to accept the things
I cannot change, the courage to change the things I can,
and the wisdom to know the difference."

—*Reinhold Niebuhr*

We ask in the Serenity Prayer for serenity to accept the things we cannot change, but how do we have serenity when we hear that someone we love is dying; or a dear friend is moving away; or we are told that we have a deadly disease or that our partner has Alzheimer's disease? In such instances we can have acceptance with bitterness, depression, sadness, but there is a lot of pain and anguish to be felt first.

Elizabeth Kübler-Ross suggests five steps to acceptance. After the initial shock, we will feel, not necessarily in this order, denial, anger, bargaining, and depression. Only then can we experience acceptance leading to serenity.

It is when we don't accept, when we think we can change reality, or when we bottle up our feelings and don't express them, or when we go over and over again the "what if's" and "if only's" that we prolong our suffering. If we are mindful of our feelings and allow ourselves to experience them, when we pray and meditate, only then can we can reach a place of balance, acceptance, and serenity inside.

Today I pray that I can find freedom and serenity by accepting life on life's terms, by accepting the things I cannot change.

"Life can be found only in the present moment.
The past is gone, the future is not yet here,
and if we do not go back to ourselves in the present
moment, we cannot be in touch with life."

—*Thich Nhat Hanh*

Looking in the mirror, seeing the body in the mirror, if I remember bodies that have looked back at me in past years, how can I not notice the changes? He used to look more youthful (younger) and now he looks older . . . his face has changed, his hair has changed color, he used to see more of his mother looking back at him and now he sees more of his father. He has a more mature look than he used to have, actually it's a more interesting face that stares back at him than before.

How marvelous to see newness and aliveness in fresh ways, to see my ancestors peeking out from my skin and eyes.

And yet, this awareness that views this body in the mirror has not changed at all. It is still fresh and clear and light, as young as a child's brightly shining mind. This mind, open to the unfolding of moment to moment experience is still so capable of enjoyment, still able to be present to the smallest shades of meaning and the largest depths of emotions. With his mind, this ever-present shining awareness, there is no aging that can be found.

—*Fred Eppsteiner*

It is a joy to be fully present and aware in this moment.

Thousands of words on aging spring to mind. Here are just a few:

- My grandmother Kane's pure white angel soft hair framing her serene face as she stood kneading the oatmeal bread.

- Dad's dread of retiring—a point at which he'd seen colleagues shrink into themselves and be bored to death.

- The simple pleasure of the senior discounts.

- Spots and wrinkles on my hands and face, and memories of how I've earned them.

- The relief of allowing myself to ask a younger, stronger person to lift the heavy clay planter, the bags of wet mulch.

- Pleasant amazement from sites from London or Tokyo in real time on TV, at digital photography, and of portable phones that also are datebooks, cameras, newspaper, tickertapes, and more.

- Realizing we probably won't have to go through another roof replacement in this lifetime . . . and that we might miss walking on the Athabasca Glacier if we don't plan fast, and that we'll never get to read all the books on our bedside tables . . . and that one of us is probably going to go first . . .

—*Jo Chaffee*

good to know

"Mindfulness can help you know what
the body needs and help you make good lifestyle
choices . . . mindfulness can help prevent
disease down the road."

—*Susan Bauer-Wu, Ph.D.*

It is well known that stress harms our immune system and mindfulness is one way to strengthen our immune system. Mindfulness also helps us to be more quickly aware of what is going on in our bodies and therefore we can seek treatment more quickly.

With the practice of mindfulness we are also more aware of our negative thoughts, which lead to depression, which leads to illness. We can stop these thoughts when we realize they are just thoughts and not reality.

*It brings me great joy to know that mindfulness
practice helps me to live a healthier life.*

It's incredible how
much younger
and lighter
I
feel
when I
let go
of
my resentments
and become
willing to
forgive.

"We have the joy of immunity from propriety now.
Like children on a beach, we can decide
whether we will wear sandals or go barefoot
through life from now on."

—*Joan Chittister*

However old we are, right now is a perfect time to stop and re-examine how we are living our lives. We can ask questions such as:

Am I living my life as I want to live it or as I think I should?

Am I really being myself or am I living out how someone else thinks I should be?

Am I being the very best me I can be?

No need for a quick answer. You might try writing down these questions and carrying them with you so you can reflect on them during the day, or put them on a table next to your bed so you can remember to think about them at the end of the day. Give them some thought, not with criticism but with curiosity.

It's never too late to change and live a richer, more satisfying life.

*I am letting the God of my understanding guide
me to have the courage to live an
authentic, honest life.*

APRIL

> "The quickest way to change your attitude
> toward pain is to accept the fact that everything
> that happens to us has been designed
> for our spiritual growth."
>
> —*M. Scott Peck*

When I was much younger I could work for hours at a time in the garden. As years went by my body would only let me spend an hour or two and then an hour. Now, after a half hour or so, I sit down to rest. I buy fewer plants at a time, knowing that they might not be planted immediately. I have to pace myself.

This is true, of course, not just with gardening. Our energy changes as years go by and we have to accept and adjust to the reality of the situation if we are going to be happy and find joy. We can struggle or deny the changes aging brings us, or we can accept the truth and learn to live with it. We always have a choice.

Today I pray to accept my life just as it is,
without resistance, but with gratitude
for the gift of each day.

Some days are for rest.
Some days are for fun.
Some days are for helping others.
Some days are for healing.
Some days are for mourning.
Some days are for silence and self-exploration.
And some days are for a mixture of all or any of this.
Each day is different.
Each and every one of us is unique.
Only you know what is right for you today.

Today, in the quiet of prayer and meditation,
I am listening to my heart and
discovering my own flow.

"Nothing is going to make us free because
only the present moment can make us free.
That realization is the awakening."

—*Eckhart Tolle*

Bring your awareness to right now, to this very moment.
This very breath is where we find joy.
Joy is right now.
Joy lies in being fully aware of our aliveness,
   our awakedness.

> *Feeel* it now
> Let yourself feel it in this moment . . .
> In this breath
> There is nothing else.

> "He who would be serene and pure needs
> but one thing, detachment."
>
> —*Meister Eckhart*

I have been practicing detachment for years, knowing intellectually that the more attached I am to anything or anybody, the more I suffer. I have tried to remember to let go of my stories and just breathe when I feel upset or my buttons are pushed.

Sometimes it works . . . sometimes not. Over the years it has improved.

BUT TODAY . . .

I really got it!!

I felt a trigger and a reaction coming up in me and

I breathed, released, and smiled

and the reaction released and I was happy

and this happened a few times . . . in seconds!

Ahhhh . . . what wonderful teachings . . .

and I am so grateful I have stayed alive long enough to learn it!

I am smiling with gratitude.

It feels so good to know I can change how I react by
simply being willing and practicing bringing my awareness
to my breath. I can let go and let God.

I don't always
know my purpose
in this world.
It is enough
to know
that
God
knows
and
I can trust
that
I will know
when
I
need to
know.

"This work of spiritual enlargement is our
common work, whether is a therapeutic setting
or in the conduct of daily life."

—*James Hollis, Ph.D.*

Deepening our connection with the God of our understanding, deepening our connection with our souls, getting to know who we really are on this journey, and following our spiritual paths brings us the greatest joy in the long run.

Some of us might need some outside help to look deeply, discover, and remove the blocks to our true nature and might want to find a therapist. Others, through personal struggle, observation, and soul-searching can find their true path.

We're never too young or too old for this journey. All it takes is the willingness to be honest and to do whatever needs to be done to remove the layers we have built over the years.

*Today I am praying for the willingness
to follow God's will for me.*

> "If you want others to be happy, practice compassion.
> If you want to be happy, practice compassion."
>
> —*His Holiness the 14th Dalai Lama*

Over the years of practice I have seen my growing capacity to sit with intense, negative thoughts and emotions such as feeling judgmental, shameful, or angry. With a mindfulness practice, these feelings become opportunities to grow into a deeper experience of living. I am not alone when I begin to see the interconnectedness with those around me.

In the workday, mindfulness settles the mind so that who I am is less about success or failures, but about listening and having conversations. Looking deeply, I see fellow workers also struggling and hoping for the same desires. As a result, when their actions bring up a familiar inner knot of judgment and irritation for me, I realize that they are bringing a lesson to me and are not out to get me. The sense of a battle to be won fades and the view of sharing a journey grows.

With a growing capacity to sit with wounds, family life changes. Seeing my parents' actions, I see the struggle in their efforts to love and realize that any pain inflicted was because of their suffering. In my adult years I also see the occasions when projections of personal hurts have caused pain for my children.

In learning to see consequences of the harm to those I most love, the patterns are clearer. To sit with this awareness in compassion, releasing anger and the personal sense of failure is freeing.

—*Marilyn Warlick*

"None of us is safe from old age,
disease, or death, for example, but most of us
can afford to feel less guarded, less braced,
and more confident in our
capacities to meet life."

—*Rick Hansen*

Today I am accepting life on life's terms.
There are some things within my control and
there are other things that I have to accept. I know,
with the help of my higher power, I am confident
I can meet all challenges without fear.

What if . . .

God's spirit is in each and every one of our hearts?

And what if, when we feel love and compassion and
generosity and joy, we are connected more deeply to
God's spirit?

And what if, when we feel anger and fear and resentment
and all the negative thoughts and emotions we have accumulated over the years, we disconnect from God's spirit?

And what if by simply bringing our awareness to our breath
and being mindful of each breath coming in and going out
we are diluting these blocks to God's spirit?

And what if, as the emotions leave,
we reconnect
with the feelings
of love and compassion and generosity and joy?

What if all this were true?
Wouldn't you want to practice
mindfulness every day?

> "The world is round and the place which
> may seem like the end may also
> be only the beginning."
>
> —*Ivy Baker Priest*

When we think about aging we might think about it as getting closer to the end of our lives. And while this is certainly true, why not think instead of how we have become wiser and more mindful of how we live each day and how we can relate in the world. We can focus on how our lives are gifts and instead of being full of fear or denial, we can think about how we can make our lives and the lives around us better.

There's a wonderful book by Karen Casey titled *Each Day a New Beginning.* This is how we should be treating each day, not by thinking about how many days we have lived or guessing how many days we still have, but focusing on TODAY, just today, and what we can do about it to make it the best today we can!

*I just have today and I am making
today the best day in my life!*

I only have this life.

I will do the best I can with this life.

I only have this day. I will do the best I can with this day.

I only have this minute. I will do the best I can with
this minute.

I only have this breath. I will do the best I can with this breath.

now

"It is only when we begin to relax with ourselves
that meditation becomes a transforming process.
Only when we relate with ourselves without
moralizing, without harshness, without deception,
can we let go of harmful patterns."

—*Pema Chödrön*

As we become more mindful, we become more relaxed and accepting of what we discover. We begin to see the harmful habits we have accumulated over the years. We can learn to stay with the feeling we have created by our own habitual thoughts and see that they are nothing more than habitual reactions to specific situations that often are formed in early childhood.

As we sit in mindfulness practice and notice what is occurring, such as boredom, anger or fear without judging or evaluating, we begin to loosen the ties they hold on us with love and acceptance.

Meditation teacher Pema Chödrön writes that we won't be free of these self-destructive patterns unless we develop a compassionate understanding of what they are. She advises that self-improvement can have temporary results, but lasting transformation occurs when we honor ourselves as the source of wisdom and compassion.

It feels so good to treat myself gently
with love and compassion.

Today I ask my heart,
"Where can I do
the most good today?"

> For the unlearned, old age is winter;
> for the learned it is the harvest.
>
> —*The Talmud*

If we think about all the things we can't do, or the things we do more slowly, or not do as well as we used to do them, our aging will feel like winter.

If, instead, we remember all we have learned and experienced and use what we have learned as we become mentors and teachers, and yes, even earth-shakers, we will be the harvesters and find joy in aging.

*It is a joy to know I can take all my experiences
and use them to help others.*

*Today I am harvesting all the richness of
my past and sharing it with others.
It feels so good to be of service.
I can find joy and purpose in my life today.*

I am taking all the time I need
to take care of myself today,
to be gentle with myself,
to listen deeply
to my inner being,
my wise self
and to flow gently
with what
I hear.

> "There are four needs in all people:
> to live, to love, to learn, to leave a legacy."
>
> —*Stephen R. Covey*

Ethical wills are a wonderful way to document our hopes and dreams, our life purpose, our values, our blessings. They can be thought of as writing a love letter to your family and close friends.

Ethical wills are not new. The Hebrew Bible first described ethical wills 3,000 years ago. References are also found in the Christian Bible and in other cultures. Initially, ethical wills were transmitted orally. Over time, they evolved into written documents. Ethical wills are not considered legal documents as compared to "living wills" and your "last will and testament," which are legal documents.

Rachael Freed, who teaches classes on ethical wills, writes that legacy writing clarifies our identity and focuses our life purpose. She says that there are six additional needs that are addressed as we write our ethical wills. "They include our need to belong, to be known, to be remembered, to have our lives make a difference, to bless and be blessed, and to celebrate Life." In her classes people invariably experience "hearty laughter and the sweet tears of amazement, gratitude, release, fullness, and a sense of peace."

Today might be a good day to begin thinking about writing an ethical will. Then, when you have more time, such as on a retreat or a quiet weekend, you can begin your writing.

*I look forward to a quiet time when I can go
deep within and begin my writing.*

"Journal keeping requires courage and sweaters.
Courage because it's often hard and painful to see your
life before you in black and white; sweaters because
we all need something to cozy up to."

—*Richard Solly*

I have frequently turned to my journal over the years as a vehicle to express what was going on in my life. Sometimes I've used it to record significant events, but most often I have journaled as a vehicle to help me through difficult times. My journal carries me from one place to another, moves me, helps me become unstuck. At various times it has served as a bridge, allowing me to leave my pain behind so that I could move on; and it has been a safe container for my feelings. It gave me great comfort and was a wonderful release.

So many things are happening to us as we age. There are losses, slow downs, downsizing, and yes, even illnesses.

Let the words and feelings come out without concern for grammar or form, or even if your thoughts don't make any sense. Let these pages serve as a safe container for your thoughts and feelings. You never have to share these words with anyone. It is up to you.

*I am willing to express all the feelings that
have been holding me back from living the joyous and
authentic life I was meant to live. I can search deep within
me and write them down in my journal, knowing
every step takes me to healing and freedom.*

time for reflections

Am I living my life with enthusiasm?
Am I continuing to learn new things and go to new places?

Today I am choosing to think about
the positive aspects of aging.

In spite of growing older . . .

Most professional athletes stop playing in the Major Leagues after their late thirties. They can still coach and play for fun, but they no longer have the speed and agility to compete with younger players. How can we expect to be any different than a professional athlete? How can we expect to be as fast and as agile as we were when we were young?

In spite of our aging bodies, we can still find many activities to enjoy well into our 80s. I see 80-year-olds working out at the gym every time I am there. People in their 80s play tennis, bowl, swim, and hike, just to name a few of the sports still available to us as we age. It's not all about shuffleboard and chess, as we often see in the movies and on television.

The first President Bush went skydiving on his 80th birthday! Author Susan Moon wrote about her mountain climbing adventures well into her 60s.

It's important to keep our body in good shape and continue to partake in the sports we love as we grow older, because once there is a lapse of time between these activities, it is harder to get back to them.

*It feels so good to have at least
one sport I love to do!*

"I don't know what your destiny will be,
but one thing I know: the only ones among you
who will be really happy are those who will
have sought and found how to serve."

—*Albert Schweitzer*

I find that meditation on a daily basis has brought me greater peace. Being at peace has enabled me to be more productive. My forty-two-plus years in recovery from alcohol addiction have given me a way of life that I would not have dreamed possible. The tools of a 12-step program have taught me how to deal with both the positive and negative happenings in life. As important have been the marvelous women and men I have met on this journey.

Although the years have taken their toll, primarily with health issues, I feel more energized spiritually, which makes me more useful to others. Service to others has helped me to grow in many ways. It has taught me patience, compassion, and understanding. It has broadened and enriched my outlook on life.

*I am grateful for the abundant
graces in my life.*

—*Jane Drury*

"Today I am taking some time to explore
what it means to live in my heart. I might journal
or meditate on this subject and get to know myself a
little better. In about the same degree as you
are helpful, you will be happy."

—*Karl Reiland*

Recently I overheard our new neighbor, 75-year-old Cliff, knock on our door and say to my husband, "I have a bum shoulder, would you help me get my arm into my shirt sleeve?" My husband obliged. As I reflected on this small act of kindness, I was reminded that each of us needs to have life supported.

I have a life blessed with basics. Sadly, many do not. But I have more. I have a circle of supportive friends who wish me well; an environment of extraordinary natural beauty and tranquility; opportunities to grow and thrive physically, spiritually, and emotionally; self-esteem; faith in a higher power; a loving family; and, at this stage in my life, I have a history. Survival no longer dominates my thoughts or my time. I can reach out to others, I can be a companion on the journey to listen, mentor, guide, and love.

—*Annette Wall*

*Today I pray I may I be open to any
opportunity to help someone.*

In spite of growing older . . .
we never have to stop learning!

K eeping our minds challenged is very important as we grow older. The more we continue to learn new things, the sharper our minds and our memories function.

If we have always enjoyed crossword puzzles, try Sudoku. If we have always enjoyed Sudoku, try crossword puzzles. There are countless brain games and puzzles available today to stimulate our minds.

People of all ages go back to school, which is a wonderful way to continue learning and also stay connected socially. Community colleges and night schools offer wonderful opportunities to learn and grow. Acquiring new skills such as a new language or even ballroom dancing have been proven to grow new neurons in our brains and thus keep our minds from becoming dull.

It's so exciting to know that no matter how old I am I can continue to learn!

"If I remembered that my breaths were numbered,
what would be my relationship
to this breath right now?"

—*Kathleen Dowling Singh*

I recently asked a friend what she thought about aging and she said she just didn't think about it. I considered this point of view. Is it better not to think about it? On the other hand, are we kidding ourselves when we say we are ignoring the fact that we are growing older? Or are we really ignoring our fears and anxieties by saying they don't exist?

Is it better to be aware of the intrinsic aging process, our being part of the natural laws and orders of the universe, and being present to our life and what it means? Don't we want to take inventory of where we have been and where we want to go with the rest of our life? Think about what is important to us and what we can let go?

*Today I am taking time to stop and
do some soul-searching so that I can make each
day the most important day of my life.*

"We can let the circumstances of our lives harden us so that we become increasingly resentful and afraid, or we can let them soften us and make us kinder and more open to what scares us. We always have this choice."

—*Pema Chödrön*

Some of us will age by becoming more cynical. We will let our lives close us down. We will remember the losses and disappointments and carry our pain, self-pity, anger, and resentments like a rock on our backs, bending us over with their weight.

Some of us will learn and grow through the events of our lives. We will be mindful of what we are going through and follow a spiritual path. We will be open and allow healing to take place.

With meditation, loving-kindness, and compassion we can be with difficult emotions. Meditation teacher Pema Chödrön writes that openness doesn't come from resisting our fears but from getting to know them well. She suggests we ask ourselves: "Do I prefer to grow up and relate to life directly, or do I choose to live and die in fear?" If we choose the former, we will come to understand that we all have pain in our lives. We will become compassionate with others and focus more on the times of joy and happiness.

We always have a choice.

God is guiding me through all the ups and downs of my life so that I may live my life fully and with an open heart.

"What do I need to accomplish so I feel my life
has accounted for something good?"

—*Pauline Payne Hardin*

It's good to stop along the way, whatever our age is right now, and take notice of how we are living our lives. We can ask ourselves: *Am I where I want to be? Am I doing what I want to do?*

If our answer is no to any of these questions we can ask ourselves what, if anything, can we do to correct the situation. If we are young enough, how can we make this happen? If not, how can we make today a day of which we are really proud?

As we learn to live our lives mindfully, more questions like these will come up for us. It's good to attend an occasional retreat and contemplate our lives. Or perhaps a day or half a day of silence in our own home will serve us well.

Another meaningful way to look deeply into these and other questions is to form a group of like-minded people and share our dreams and our concerns. This can be healing and inspirational.

*I am making a plan today to explore how
I can live my life with purpose.*

"The Constitution doesn't guarantee happiness, only the
pursuit of it. You have to catch up to it yourself."

—Author Unknown

Author Mac Anderson once asked a cab driver, "If you could
live anywhere in the world—and if money was no object—
where would you live?" Without hesitating even for a second, he
replied, "I live in my heart. So it really doesn't matter where my
body lives. If I am happy inside, then I live in paradise, no matter
where my residence is."

This sounds so simple, but how do we live in our hearts? To
me, living in my heart happens when I feel love, compassion, forgiveness, or gratitude. I am living there when I feel any of these
feelings myself or observe them in someone else. I remember
one day stopping at a red light and seeing a father waiting at the
bus stop for his child to come home from school. The minute the
little boy jumped off the bus he ran into his father's open arms. I
could feel my heart expand and warmth spread across my chest.
My eyes filled with tears and the driver behind me honked when
the light turned green. I was lost in the beauty of the moment.

Living in our hearts requires our being present to the hearts
of others. Living in our hearts means we are mindful so that we
can catch a precious moment like this one, so that we are open to
touch another person when we feel their pain.

*Today my heart is open to receive love and
compassion and this fills me with joy.*

"When we let go of our battles and open our hearts to things as they are, then we come to rest in the present moment. This is the beginning and end of spiritual practice."

—*Jack Kornfield*

The technique of noting or labeling is very helpful. In mindfulness we learn to label our thoughts as they appear in our minds and then go back to our breathing. By labeling them, or naming them, we are acknowledging and accepting them, rather than resisting or fighting them. An example of this is when a thought or a plan comes into our mind, we simply say, "Thinking" or "Planning." Noting helps us accept our thoughts and then let them go.

Once, while on an airplane, I was writing. I became very frustrated at another passenger's loud music. I remembered noting. So then I thought, "Disturbing music," and "Interruption" and after a moment, as I accepted the fact that I could do nothing about the music, it went more into the background and I became completely absorbed with my writing.

Jack Kornfield writes, "Naming the difficulties we encounter brings clarity and understanding and can unlock and free the valuable energy locked up in them."

It is so good to know that when I am disturbed by a thought, I can stop, name what I am feeling, and be at peace.

"Keeping hearts happy is a lot like keeping
bodies healthy. We need to feed our hearts well
through reading, prayer, and meditation,
and exercise them by loving."

—*Jan Nakken*

Reading inspirational and spiritual literature before our mindfulness meditation in the morning helps us because it encourages positive and loving thoughts throughout the day. It keeps us on a spiritual path. As we meditate on the words we have read, our hearts are storing the feelings these words evoke. They are with us, whether we are aware of them or not. At any time during the day, we can trigger them by an act or thought of love, compassion, or generosity.

Each morning, as I take time to read, meditate,
and pray, I am deepening my connection with God.
This helps me to be open to God's guidance,
finding opportunities to practice being a
loving and compassionate person.

Taking a Shower

Adding a new practice of being fully aware of taking a shower helps us develop our practice of mindfulness. We are learning to be aware of each moment, to be fully alive in each moment rather than letting our minds drift off into the past or the future. Each day make an intention to be with the total experience of taking a shower.

> Bring your awareness to your breath. If at any time you find yourself off in a thought or a daydream, just bring your awareness back to the moment.
>
> Feel your hand on the faucet as you turn on the water.
>
> Listen to the sound of the water.
>
> Feel your hand on your soap and watch how it changes as you put it under the water.
>
> Smell the scent of the soap.
>
> Be fully aware of the soap as you wash all parts of your body.
>
> Hear the change of the sound as you wash off the soap.
>
> Listen to the silence as you turn off the water.
>
> Be aware of the feeling of the towel as you dry yourself.
>
> Enjoy the peace.
>
> As you develop this habit you will soon find it easier to bring this practice of mindfulness to other activities of your day.

MAY

"Fifty years: here's a time when you have to
separate yourself from what other people expect
of you, and do what you love. Because if you find
yourself 50 years old and you aren't doing
what you love, then what's the point?"

—*Jim Carrey*

As I recently turned 50 years old I am surprised at how calm and peaceful I am with the age. I have great hopes that this half of my life will be happier, more serene, and full of fun and excitement. I know for these things to happen I have to make changes in my life. I am ready to make the changes I have been discussing with my higher power, knowing it is the right path for me to take.

—*Debbie Boisseau*

*It's exciting to know that
my life is continuing to be full and
rich as I stay open to new and
exciting experiences.*

"This work of spiritual enlargement is
our common work, whether in a therapeutic
setting or in the conduct of daily life."

—*James Hollis, Ph.D.*

Deepening our connection with the God of our understanding, deepening our connection with our souls, getting to know who we really are on this journey, and following our spiritual paths brings us the greatest joy in the long run.

Some of us might need some outside help to look deeply, discover, and remove the blocks to our true nature and might want to find a therapist. Others, through personal struggle, observation, and soul-searching, can find their true path.

We're never too young or too old for this journey. All it takes is the willingness to be honest and to do whatever needs to be done to remove the layers we have built over the years.

Today I am praying for the willingness
to follow God's will for me.

I am not who I was yesterday,
last week, or last year.
I am not who I will be tomorrow,
next week, or next year.
I pray to know what I can do today
to make this
the most important day
of my life.

"I would love to live like the river flows,
carried by the surprise of its
own unfolding."

—*John O'Donohue*

I am learning to be present
in this moment
right now
letting life flow
by itself
and
filling me
with
joy.

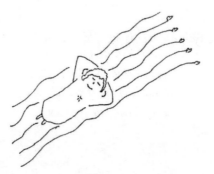

> "I don't think we can postpone meditation
> until we move or clean out the garage!"
>
> *—Eknath Easwaran*

If we want to live a life of meaning as we grow older, one way is to take time for mindful meditation. We need to stop and take twenty minutes or so each morning to train our minds to be in the present moment. We need to stop and connect with the God of our understanding.

Even if you usually get up at 5:30 or 6:00 AM and think, by getting up twenty minutes earlier, that you will be tired, know that you won't be. Many years ago I learned that twenty minutes of meditation is equivalent to two hours of sleep. I have found this to be true for over thirty years.

Beginning our day with meditation helps us to live richer and fuller lives. By learning to bring our full awareness to each moment, to be fully alive in each moment to all there is, will be well worth getting up twenty minutes earlier!

I am so grateful that I am making
mindfulness a part of my life today.
It is giving me such joy!

with the help of
mindfulness

*I can accept exactly where I am
in my life and find joy.*

"Meditation is a way of quieting the mind so you
can practice all day long, wherever you are; seeing where
there is grasping or aversion, clinging or suffering;
and then let it go . . . a resting in awareness."

—*Ajahn Chah*

Often we are not aware of what feelings we are carrying within us which block us from feeling joy. We just wonder what's wrong with us or with our world.

It's good to stop occasionally and take a personal inventory. Examine what it is that is keeping you from feeling at one with others, keeping you separated from God. You might want to ask yourself some questions. Sit quietly, spend a few moments with your breath, and then ask yourself questions such as:

Am I holding on to anger or resentments? Is there something I am afraid of? Am I getting enough exercise? Am I shutting myself off from seeing friends? Am I doing something new?

It is good to spend some time after this meditation writing down what you found in a journal or writing a letter to God. Then talk to a trusted friend or a member of the clergy or a therapist.

Mindfulness can be like shining a light in our dark corners and uncovering the layers that are keeping us from happiness and contentment.

*Today I am taking all the time I need to stop and look deeply,
discovering my blocks that keep me from feeling joy and peace.*

"Mindfulness is the aware, balanced acceptance
of the present experience. It isn't more complicated than
that. It is the opening to or receiving the present moment,
pleasant or unpleasant, just as it is, without
either clinging to it or rejecting it."

—*Sylvia Boorstein*

Mindfulness is one of the many forms of meditation. We use the term "the practice of mindfulness" or "the practice of meditation" because it is simply that, a practice. Just as we practice the piano, dancing, or anything that requires repetition to gain skills, we practice mindfulness by sitting with our breath, noticing what takes us away from our breath, and returning to our breath for one or more periods each day.

Its purpose is to be fully awake and aware in each moment, to discover the essence of who we are, and to get in touch with all the blocks that keep us from touching our inner spirit and listening to the guidance of our soul.

Author Pema Chödrön writes that "Everything in our lives can help us to wake up or to fall asleep, and basically it's up to us to let it wake us up."

Today I am practicing being fully awake!
I am bringing my awareness into everything I do.

"With our mindful breath and mindful steps
we can produce the energy of mindfulness and return to
the awakened wisdom lying in each cell of our body."

—*Thich Nhat Hanh*

Many of us have unfinished business from early childhood. We have feelings that are stuffed and locked inside us, keeping us from being free and happy. These emotions come from memories that are stored in what is often called our inner child.

Mindfulness is a wonderful way to heal our inner child and thus experience more joy as we age. Our inner child may be wounded from neglect, from being misunderstood, and from not getting our early needs met. We may have anger and pain stored so deeply inside that we are not even aware that it is there. Mindfulness is like a light shining on the dark places that need healing.

In order for us to heal, we first have to acknowledge that this pain exists. When we are quiet in mindfulness meditation, we can look deeply and find our inner child. Then we can embrace our inner child, telling her or him that we are there for them— that whatever happened in the past wasn't the fault of our inner child, and we are there to take care of them now. We give ourselves lots of love and compassion and gradually find that we are more open and in less pain. If this is too difficult for you to do alone, a good therapist can be of great help.

*I am filled with love and compassion today as I embrace
my inner child and help myself heal.*

"We'll never make perfect decisions, and wanting to
make the perfect choice keeps us paralyzed."

—*Leo Babauta*

Decision-making does not necessarily get easier as we age. One technique I have found very helpful over the years is guided imagery. First, meditate to become calm and centered. Then, let yourself imagine one of your choices. For example, if you are thinking about downsizing, imagine first staying where you are. Imagine all that this means to you. For example, can you handle it financially? Let yourself feel all this. Would you rather use your money for other things? Imagine downsizing. How would that feel? Let yourself sit with your choices. Don't rush.

Then when you feel you have felt it all, sit quietly with a pen and paper and jot down what you found. It is helpful to allow at least twenty-four hours to go by without making a decision. It might not give us the perfect answer, but it can help us to get in touch with our feelings, which can lead us to a decision that feels right.

You can pray about it and trust you will be guided in the right direction. And if you don't need to know right away, stop thinking about it and let your subconscious or your intuition take over. Very often, when we let go of the struggle of trying to make a decision, the answers are suddenly here.

*Today I trust that God is guiding me to the right answer
and I will know what to do when the time is right.*

"Keeping hearts happy is a lot like keeping
bodies healthy. We need to feed our hearts well
through reading, prayer, and meditation,
and exercise them by loving."

—*Jan Nakken*

Reading inspirational and spiritual literature before our mindfulness meditation in the morning helps us because it encourages positive and loving thoughts throughout the day. It keeps us on a spiritual path. As we meditate on the words we have read, our hearts are storing the feelings these words evoke. They are with us, whether we are aware of them or not. At any time during the day, we can trigger them by an act or thought of love, compassion, or generosity.

*Each morning, as I take time to read, meditate,
and pray, I am deepening my connection with God.
This helps me to be open to God's guidance,
finding opportunities to practice being a loving
and compassionate person.*

"Whether you're up or you're down,
whether you're confident or unsure,
listen to your heart.
For your heart knows why you're here."

—*Ralph Marston*

As we grow older, there are going to be days, weeks, months, or even longer when we experience a variety of physical, mental, and spiritual states. Actually, this happened when we were younger as well, but the ones in our future may be more difficult to go through. There are more aches and pains, more limitations, more losses.

No matter what we are going through, there is a purpose for us on this planet. Mindfulness helps us to trust our inner guidance. Mindfulness helps us to follow our spiritual path.

*I connect with my Higher Power in my
morning prayer and meditation and know
that I am being led on my journey.*

good to know

Studies show the emotional support we get
from friends and loved ones in our relationships has a
positive effect on our immune, hormonal, and
cardiovascular systems, can lower blood pressure and
cholesterol, and ultimately helps us live longer.

Research also tells us that some of the values of having strong, meaningful relationships are that we have less susceptibility to disease, have an increased survival rate from heart attack, live a longer, healthier life, wake up with more hopefulness and a positive outlook, have increased vitality and zest, and life has greater meaning, purpose, and richness.

*I am so grateful for the friends and loved ones
I have in my life today. I pray that I may always be
considerate and thoughtful and appreciate and
return the love I receive from them.*

"He who has so little knowledge of
human nature as to seek happiness by changing
anything but his own disposition will
waste his life in fruitless efforts."

—*Samuel Johnson*

My physical therapist told me how inspiring her patients are. Many are in their 80s and 90s and are still active with a rich and fulfilling life. She said that she sees how people get out of life what they really want and that many are still looking for the same things that someone half their age would.

Why not spend some time today to look at what your expectations are about your life.

Are they too high, too low, or realistic?

If they are too high, you will often be disappointed.

If they are too low, you'll miss out on many opportunities.

How do they make you feel?

> *Today I am putting into life what I want*
> *out of it so I trust the outcomes.*

time for reflections

"Mindfulness is probably one of the most powerful stress busters out there. It's also a phenomenal way to become fully engaged with life. Practiced and taught by teachers in traditions ranging from Vedic and Tantric to Buddhist and everything in between, it's a versatile practice that we often gain access to through meditation, but can easily transfer to everyday living."

—*Lindsey Lewis*

Here are just a few ways to be mindful in everyday living:

- Meditate first every morning.
- Bring your awareness to brushing your teeth and taking a shower.
- Bring your full attention to cooking your meals.
- Stay mindful while eating. Turn off the television and refrain from reading anything.
- Give full attention to any conversation you have.
- Take a mindful walk sometime during the day or evening.
- End your day being mindful of all the things for which you are grateful.

Now add some more ideas of your own.

Today
I am
going to
let
this day
take me wherever
it wants
me to
go

> "What do I need to accomplish so I feel my
> life has accounted for some good?"
>
> —*Paula Payne Harden*

Whatever our age, it is good to stop at some point along the way and take note of where we are on our spiritual path. We can sit quietly, still our minds, and ask ourselves some sincere questions.

Am I where I want to be?

Am I doing what I want to do?

If you hesitate or say no to any of these questions, ask yourself:

What do I really want to do with my life?

Is there any way I can make this happen?

If that answer is no, ask:

Can I accept my present situation for now?

If you are young enough, ask:

How can I make this happen?

If you are not, ask:

How can I make today a day I am proud of?

> *Before I start my day today I am taking time to*
> *pray I can make it a day well lived.*

FEAR =
False Evidence Appearing Real

Any fears we might have about growing older are just projections, concerns about something that hasn't happened yet. It is possible that we might live to the ripe old age of 100 and still be healthy, or we could be hit by a bus tomorrow. Why waste time and energy worrying about something that isn't here? Why let yourself become stressed about the unknown? Some think stress creates disease and we can actually, by our thoughts, create that which we fear the most.

When fears of aging come to you, mindfully ask yourself if you are doing all you can to be healthy today.

Are you eating properly?

Are you getting enough exercise?

Are you taking care of yourself mentally, physically, and spiritually?

If not, make a plan to add these into your life. If you are doing them already, wonderful!

*I am keeping my attention on being
in today and enjoying it!*

mindful in nature

"All Nature wears one universal grin."
—*Tom Thumb the Great*

Getting lost in nature can be so enriching, and it can heal our mind, body, and spirit. But what happens if we can't get outside? What if we have to work for a living, take care of a sick friend or relative, or stay in with the child who has chicken pox? What happens when we are sick or the weather is stormy? We can bring nature to us in a number of ways, maybe not quite as satisfyingly as being out of doors, but certainly fulfilling and relaxing.

There are many ways we can connect with nature and experience its greatness, even indoors. Outside gardens can offer peace and joy from a window view. Take a few moments to water your plants, repot an overgrown plant, or watch the leaves or rain or snow outside your window. Plant seeds and grow an indoor garden. Force bulbs and feel the joy of their bloom long before they break through the earth outdoors. Build a terrarium. Add a greenhouse to your kitchen window. Grow herbs on your kitchen windowsill. I feel uplifted and excited every time I cut dill from my own plant to use in a recipe.

Whether we have five minutes or five hours, whether we are inside or outside, we can find time to be mindful in solitude and in nature.

I can add to the ways I can connect with nature indoors,
preparing myself for the days when I can't go out.

"Yes, it's a good day for singing a song, and
it's a good day for moving along.
Yes, it's a good day, how could anything go wrong.
A good day from morning 'til night."

—*Peggy Lee*

This is a great time to be older. I often wish I could show my mother and my grandmother how much easier it is to be productive and happy, now, as an older woman. When I throw the laundry into the washer and dryer, I remember my mother scrubbing at the washboard. I remember how on rainy Mondays we ran to pull the laundry in from the clothesline and the wet wash would hang around for days, waiting for sunshine to return.

My grandmother would be amazed to learn that my hips are artificial, and that medicine has saved my life three times. I would show my mother how much easier the computer has made my life, enabling me to write for hours despite my arthritic hands and corrects my errors and makes copies without messy carbon paper, correction tape, or white-out, how it even tells me when I've spelled a word wrong, even though it looks okay to me.

I am older now than my grandmother was when she died after several years of being an invalid, because we didn't know much about nutrition, and we didn't know that physical therapy could get her back on her feet.

I'm back on my feet, eating carefully, and exercising gently, still participating in life.

—*Samantha M. White*

Today I am grateful to be alive and for all that I still can do.

did you know?

"I have to exercise in the morning before my
brain figures out what I'm doing."

—*Marsha Doble*

Exercise helps people feel and function better mentally and physically. It becomes more and more important as we age, and yet, for many people, it becomes harder. Even knowing how important it is does not make it an easy or fun thing to do. It takes discipline but it's worth it. Exercise can:

- Keep older people active
- Make the frailest people stronger
- Make the heart stronger
- Improve circulation and decreases blood pressure
- Boost the immune system

As much as you might not want to exercise, there is no denying its value. So, instead of thinking of all the reasons to put it off, remember positive affirmations such as these:

*It feels so good to exercise regularly.
I am exercising and getting
healthier every day.*

Our breath

·

·

this breath

·

·

brings us back
to
ourselves

·

·

now

·

·

in this moment

·

·

Which is perfect

now

"Live today because tomorrow is not promised."

—*Author unknown*

I remember an incident when friends asked if my partner and I would like to go kayaking with them next spring. My partner immediately said she wasn't up to it while I enthusiastically answered yes! I overheard my partner whisper something.

"What did she say?" I asked.

One friend laughed, "She said, 'Ruth doesn't know that she's 62.'"

The truth was, I didn't identify the age 62 as old. And I don't identify with the age I am now as old. I knew I was "getting older," but I felt relatively healthy and capable and I had good energy, as I do today. It was true that I couldn't do all the things I could do 10 or 20 years earlier.

Then one day a piece of tissue paper flew over a wall no more than two feet high. Rather than just climbing up and jumping down without giving it a thought, something inside of me said, *Be careful.* I observed an argument between my cautious self and my carefree "I can do anything" self. My cautious self won, and I walked to the end of the wall and around, picked up the tissue paper, and walked back. A definite sign of my awareness of aging, I must admit.

As we age, our issues change. Although our inner spirit ideally continues to grow freer and more spiritually connected, our physical bodies develop limitations that prevent us from doing everything we would like to do, as I had discovered at the wall. Losses, limitations, changing times, pain, and diminished energy all sneak up on us. How we look at life changes. What was important last year might be less important today.

I am fully enjoying my life within the limits of my abilities.

> "Smiling is infectious; you can catch it like the flu.
> Someone smiled at me today, and I started smiling too."
>
> —*Author unknown*

I used to be a busy social worker and loved my work. After a move that made it possible for my husband to keep his job, I couldn't find one. Unexpectedly, I was retired.

With the help of our dog, Raja, a golden retriever, I found my new mission. Raja and I visit patients on the cardiac floor of a nearby hospital. One day I came into a room and the patient was lying in her bed in such discomfort she could barely muster the energy to talk or move. I squatted by the bed and asked her softly if she'd like a visit from a dog. She said, "Yes." As soon as Raja came to her bedside she turned toward him and began to pat his head and scratch behind his ears. Love shone in her eyes. A smile brightened her face.

Another day I entered a room where the woman lying in bed was as thin as a stick. She had no teeth and every inch of her skin was wrinkled. I almost gasped. I told her about Raja, now waiting in the hall. "Yes," she said, and her smile was so beautiful I felt as if I'd been warmed by the sun. Once the visit was over she smiled again and said, "God bless you, and thank you for coming." It was an encounter that was so sweet and so uplifting I'll never forget it.

I've learned that I can feel happy from something as brief as a smile. The world needs many, many smiles in order to be a safer and less violent place. Each time we smile we move the world closer to peace.

—*Susan Gnosh*

I feel so much better when I smile!

"Our problems are opportunities to
discover God's solutions."

—*Author unknown*

There are times when we are suffering and we can't seem to
find any joy or happiness in our lives. Perhaps a loved one
has died or we just heard that we have a serious disease. Perhaps
we don't know where we're going to get the money for unex-
pected expenses. Any number of reasons can put us into a feeling
of depression.

Rather than running away from our feelings, we can acknowledge them. Rather than rushing around trying to fix them, cover
them up, or deny them, we can give ourselves lots of love.

Loving-kindness is a wonderful way to take care of ourselves
with gentleness and love. We can sit quietly and bring our awareness to where we feel love, where our heart lives. Then we can
think of something that makes us feel loving, such as holding
a kitten or a newborn baby. When we are quiet, we can say to
ourselves:

May I be happy.
May I be peaceful.
May I be healed.
May I be free from suffering.

We can breathe in peace and calm as we say these words to
ourselves. No matter what is going on in our lives, we can surround ourselves with loving thoughts and release our suffering.

Today I trust that God is taking care of me
as I becoming willing to turn over all my suffering.

"Nothing really dies," I told him.
"It just turns into something else. Everything is always
changing form. Do you remember the pumpkin that
rotted into the earth in your garden? Tomatoes sprouted
where it used to be. This bird will go back to the earth
and turn into lavender flowers and butterflies."

—*Anne Cushman*

At different times in our lives we come to the realization that we are not going to live forever. When I asked friends how old they were when they came to this understanding I received many answers. Somewhere in the 50s seem to be the most common. One friend who was 50 said she realized she had less life to go than she had lived. It made her feel sad because of the lack of success she thought she had achieved and the years she had wasted.

Another friend was 40 and he said, "I remember the shock, realizing that 'someday' had already passed, and that I was most likely halfway done." Another realized that life was limited when he was 51 and his dad passed away. His reaction was that he had better start living his life and do what gives him joy. Almost everyone believed that it was important to have a purpose in their lives.

No matter at what age we realize that we aren't going to live forever, it's so important not to look back with regret, but to look forward to aging with joy and purpose. We can make our life something we are proud of from this day on. Whatever time we have left of our life left to live, we can make it something for which we have no regrets.

I am making today the best today I can make it!

my practice

Brushing My Teeth

Our minds are usually on other things when we are doing something routine, such as brushing our teeth. We might be going over our to-do list or worried about something. Brushing our teeth is a wonderful way to practice mindfulness. Each day make an intention to be with the total experience of brushing your teeth. Bring your awareness to your breath. If at any time you find yourself in a thought or a daydream, just bring your awareness back to the moment.

Feel your hand on the faucet as you turn on the water.

Listen to the sound of the water.

Feel your hand on your toothbrush and the toothpaste tube.

Smell the toothpaste.

Be aware as you put the toothpaste onto your brush.

Notice what it feels like when you put the brush into your mouth.

Notice the taste.

Feel the water in your mouth.

Stay with the movements of your hand as you brush your teeth.

Listen to the silence as you turn off the water.

Enjoy the peace.

As you develop this habit you will soon find it easier to bring this practice of mindfulness to others activities of your day.

What happiness is there in waking
to a new day, a new idea
if old memories and failures
squeeze through all the open spaces
crowd out the sunrise
what is the point of walking the beach
if I can't see the tide
going out or coming in
washing old stuff away
delivering surprises

—Vivian Plenge

*Today I will watch to see the light of a new day
and release old memories to the tide.*

"When a man does not know what harbor he
is making for, no wind is the right wind."

—Seneca the Younger

I have experienced the joy of connecting with many beautiful people in my classes, workshops, and retreats. Many of them have opened their hearts and shared their deepest fears, resentments, pains, and longings, and together we have created affirmations to move forward to the next step in their lives.

In one workshop a woman told us she didn't know what to do with her life now that she was retired and found no interest in anything anymore. An 84-year-old woman and her husband sold their family business that they had worked in together for 60 years. Soon after, he died and she no longer wanted to get out of bed in the morning.

I suggested that she write the following affirmation 10 times a day for 21 days: "God is guiding me to my next step to increase joy and purpose in my life."

Affirmations are simple, positive statements we put out into the universe and open ourselves up to receiving positive energy back. Within weeks the woman emailed me, describing how she felt more at peace and hopeful.

My heart is guiding me to my life's work. It feels so good to trust that God is revealing a plan for me, one day at a time.

> "All my life through, the new sights
> of Nature made me rejoice like a child."
>
> —*Marie Curie*

I was sitting outside on my deck one day when I heard my mind say: "What are you going to do, just sit and watch the tomatoes grow?"

"No." I said. "I'm just checking on the tomatoes. I'm noticing that they're a little bigger today than they were yesterday." Nothing else. I was at total peace. Sometimes I simply sit and stare at the waves coming in and out at the beach, or at ripples in a pond, or leaves fluttering like tiny dancers in the slightest breeze. I can become lost simply watching a baby or a puppy play, a butterfly soar or a bumblebee flit from blossom to blossom.

"I'm going out to check the flowers," I'd say to no one in particular and out I go, studying each flower, checking for growth, or their need for water, all the while marveling at how beautiful they are.

Rachel Carson tells us that "Those who dwell, as scientists or laymen, among the beauties and mysteries of the earth are never alone or weary of life . . . Those who contemplate the beauty of the earth find reserves of strength that will endure as long as life lasts."

Becoming mindful of nature's tiny details, being totally aware with all our senses for just a few minutes, can restore balance to a scattered mind, rest and healing to our bodies, and joy to our spirits.

> *Today I will take at least five minutes, more if I can,*
> *to rest my mind and my body experiencing nature.*
> *I will take time to get better acquainted with nature.*

I celebrate all of me today!
Weaknesses and strengths alike!
I celebrate every part of me
And
I
feel
JOY!

JUNE

my practice

"It's not how many times we go away
from our breathing, but how many times
we come back that counts."

—*Thich Nhat Hanh*

Please don't think you are meditating wrong when you find yourself off in a daydream or a plan or making a shopping list. Your mind is used to going in all these directions and many more. Mindful meditation is a training, a practice.

When your mind drifts away, simply notice it, label it, such as thinking or planning, and come back to your breathing. Repeat this ... again and again ... for as many agains as it takes. Labeling helps to release the thought and makes it easier to come back to your breathing.

Eventually there will be fewer and fewer mind excursions and your mind will quiet down. Not always. Usually.

Tara Brach suggests that when we get lost we need only pause, look at what is true, relax our heart and arrive again.

*It feels so good to sit, breathe, and watch my mind
do what it wants to do until eventually it does what
I want it to do—rest in the present moment.*

Breathing in to all the
aches and pains in my body
I am releasing
my
tension
Breathing in to all the
aches and pains in my body
I am softening
my pain
Breathing in
Breathing out
I am feeling better

good news

S cientists tell us that people with pets tend to move around more, suffer less depression, and have higher survival rates after having a heart attack. There are many articles that show the benefits to elderly persons are tenfold. Pets lower blood pressure and pulse rate. People with pets have 21 percent fewer visits to the doctor. They find it easier to make friends and seniors become more active. Pets offer affection and unconditional love.

Loneliness is one of the greatest fears we have for growing older. Pets ease loss of a loved one and fight loneliness. People play with their pets, talk to their pets, confide in their pets. The list goes on and on.

So love your pet. Hug your pet. And above all, if you don't have one, get a pet!

What the Years Have Taught Me

I am not the center of the universe.

I can actually leave the house without make-up.

Wearing comfortable clothes and shoes is more important
than being stylish.

I dress for me and not for "them."

I don't know who "them" are anyway.

I no longer scream when I see my mother's face every time
I look in the mirror.

I realize that Moms knew what they were talking about.

Peace and love are more important to me than money and
possessions.

Peace and love can only be transmitted when they exist in me.

True friends love you even when you are wrong.

I do not take myself too seriously anymore.

A sense of humor and forgiveness can get me through almost
anything.

Life is a gift that sure beats the alternative.

—*Shirley Smith*

"We can do no great things,
only small things with great love."

—*Mother Teresa*

Envision something you can do for others.

It can be something you do well that has helped you in your life
that you

Can share with others . . .

Or some skill that you can teach.

Perhaps you feel drawn to another way to help

Such as volunteering to read to the blind

Or be a big brother or big sister.

Look deeply and find a path of service

Or stay on the path you are on as long as it brings you satisfaction

And you will have joy in your life at every age!

"When the Japanese mend broken objects,
they aggrandize the damage by filling the cracks
with gold. They believe that when something's
suffered damage and has a history it
becomes more beautiful."

—*Barbara Bloom*

Can we look at our own history like this?
Can we find strength in our failures?
  Our imperfections?
Can we accept our disappointments?
  Our losses?
Can we celebrate our successes?
  Our joys?
Can we love our progress?
  Our goodness?

*Today I am treating my entire life gently,
with love and compassion, knowing that every single
thing I have done is a part of the wonderful,
miraculous human being that I am.*

eggs
peanut butter
hot choc
Australia?
Antarctica??

Writer Raymond Carver died of lung cancer in 1988 at the age of 50. This errand list was found in his shirt pocket after his death.

From the mundane to the extraordinary, what's important on your to-do list? Why not take some time today to explore this?

*Today I am stopping to take time to
explore what is important in my life and do
my best to live with this in mind.*

"May I mindfully acknowledge that others,
like myself, are still growing spiritually, and forgive
their past offenses, as I forgive my own, so I can
know the blessings of a loving heart."

—*Jean Smith*

Over the years many of us have accumulated resentments that we might not even remember. They don't surface unless something triggers the incident that caused the resentment. The more we hold on to these memories, the more blocked we are from feeling joy. Once we realize resentments do us more harm than the person or situation that we resent, we can pray for the willingness to let go. Thich Nhat Hanh illustrates this very well when he gives the following example:

> Imagine you are going to throw a hot, burning coal at someone with whom you are angry. Imagine what that coal is doing to your hand!

Why not make a general intention to be free from all resentments! Make a clean slate and forgive everyone, including ourselves.

*It feels so good to be entirely ready to have
God remove all my resentments and help me forgive
all past offenses, including my own, so that I
can know the blessings of a loving heart.*

> "To be conscious that we are perceiving or
> thinking is to be conscious of
> our own existence."
>
> *—Aristotle*

I magine something coming up in the future that makes you nervous. Perhaps you are making a presentation or having an operation. Feel how your body responds to these thoughts. Are you holding your breath? Does your stomach tighten or turn over? Where do you hold your fears?

Now bring your attention to a time when you felt great joy. Again, feel how your body responds to this memory. Is there a different expression on your face? Is your body more relaxed? Is your breath different?

By bringing our awareness to these feelings, they tend to lose their power over us. When we open up to the awareness of the present moment, and breathe into it, the feelings wash away and we can feel peace.

We can train ourselves to be mindful and thus be happier, healthier, and more joyful as we age.

Today I am taking time to be aware of how I respond
to my thoughts and feelings. I am being gentle
and loving with myself, however I feel.

"When we truly rest in awareness, our
experience is spacious and intimate, without defenses.
With it arises compassion; we feel our heart's
natural compassion with life."

—*Jack Kornfield*

One of the most important results of practicing mindfulness
is having compassion for ourselves. As we learn to observe
and not judge that which is going on in the present moment,
we become gentler with ourselves. For example, when anger or
jealousy comes up, we can simply notice it. We can feel it in our
body but not act on it. We can breathe in and out three times and
watch it soften within us and begin to lose its energy. Soon we
learn to do the same with all our feelings and emotions, all our
memories, and all our imperfections and mistakes in the present
moment.

As we become more compassionate, forgiving, and loving
with ourselves we are experiencing more joy in our lives.

*It feels so wonderful to become more and
more joyful as my heart softens and becomes
filled with love and compassion.*

Let go of the past.
Don't project into the future.
Live in this moment.
It's actually
this simple
and
yet

.

.

.

not so easy!
Make it a goal.
An intention.
It works.

"Life is denied by lack of attention,
whether it be to cleaning windows or
trying to write a masterpiece."

—*Nadia Boulanger*

How many times have you been driving and suddenly realized that you didn't remember driving from one place to another? How often do you find yourself in a conversation suddenly realizing that you haven't heard part of what the speaker was saying to you? Your mind has been either off in a daydream, or wondering what you are going to say next, or judging what is being said to you. Maybe it went away remembering something in the past or worried about something coming up in the future?

A daily practice of meditation helps to develop concentration and focus. It helps to train your mind to be in the moment, to bring your full attention to what is going on in the moment. You can become a better listener and a friend by totally being present with another person.

Mindfulness is a wonderful way to end our stress, fear, and the ways we create suffering in our lives.

*It is so powerful to know that I can bring
more peace and love into my life by practicing meditation.
I am learning to become gentle and loving with myself.
I am learning to let go of my suffering.*

Sit quietly and bring your awareness to your breath.
Now imagine a time in your life when you felt joy. Perhaps
 when you first learned how to ride a bicycle or swim or when
 you fell in love or when you held a newborn baby.
Let that feeling flow all through you and over you.
Feel it in all the cells in your body.
Breathe joy in.
Breathe joy out.
Now spread that feeling to all the memories you have of your past.
Whatever actually happened doesn't matter.
You've survived all these years and you are here now.
Let joy spread everywhere . . . like a rainbow . . .
Spreading over you and spreading over all the years you lived,
 bathing you through all the hard times
 all the good times
 all the failures
 all the successes
 like a gentle breeze on a beautiful sunny day.
Watch as your heart is flooded with joy
 as you breathe in joy
 as you breathe out joy
 filling . . . emptying . . .
Sit this way for as long as you want.
Know that you can come back to this feeling anytime.
Feel the joy.[1]

---

[1] *You might want to make a recording of this meditation so you can play it back and experience it with your eyes closed.*

Take some time today to smile at the person you see in the mirror.

If you see lines or wrinkles . . .

Just smile.

If you see a few gray hairs or all gray hair or no hair at all . . .

Just smile.

If you see a face with worry or pain

Just smile.

If you see some of your mother's or father's face . . .

Just smile.

Let your heart soften.

Send love and compassion to the you in the mirror

And

say

I love you!

good to know

Studies have proven that mindfulness improves heart health. Did you know studies have proven that dark chocolate improves heart health, too?

*I will do something fun
for myself today!*

"Seeing, hearing, feeling are miracles, and
each part and tag of me is a miracle."

—*Walt Whitman*

Sometimes I realize that my being alive is a miracle. More so the older I get. And when I do, I like to stop whatever I am doing and thinking and just be aware 100 percent of my breathing in and out. For me, another miracle. Do I live in a world of miracles?

—*William Menza*

*Looking deeply, I am aware of my breath
coming in and going out and I know it is a gift.
My breath is a gift. I am a miracle.*

"God isn't through with me yet."

—*Old saying*

Most of the time I truly am filled with gratitude. Although I don't like the number it says on my license I am so grateful to have been able to accomplish the dreams I have lived. Certainly the years have taught me about patience, kindness, tolerance, and unconditional love. God has gifted me many times over. Along with the good, there is always the ability to feel and experience pain and hurt and fear, but my faith continues to walk me through a lot of it. Prayer is a relief and an unburdening of things I have no power over. In truth I still feel that pain, but it doesn't paralyze me as it once did.

—*Diane Crosby*

I am so grateful that I can turn over everything for which I am powerless and know that God is guiding me to peace.

> "The most basic of all human needs is the need
> to understand and be understood. The best way to
> understand people is to listen to them."
>
> —*Ralph Nichols*

Let's begin with listening to ourselves. This is the only way we can understand ourselves. Listen to your heart. What are you feeling right now? What does your heart need? What can you give it? If no one else was around and you just had yourself to fulfill your needs, what would you do? What would you say?

Listen to your body. What is it feeling right now? Does it need exercise? A better menu? Can you love your body just the way it is and take good care of it?

When we really listen deeply, open our hearts to our own needs, the needs of our hearts and our bodies, then we can be a better listener to others. When we can listen to ourselves without rationalization and justification, without negativity and judgments, we can take this practice into our conversation with others. As we truly listen, we are filled with the peace and love that comes with understanding and accepting ourselves and others.

Today I am taking time to really be
here with my heart, my mind, and my ears.
I am putting aside all judgments as I just listen with
compassion and understanding and acceptance.

Today I am choosing
to be loving
and compassionate
to every ache and pain
in my body.
Rather than tensing
and disliking my pain
and making it worse,
I am softening
and relaxing
and breathing
into them.
I am feeling
love and compassion
and appreciation for
all of me,
every part of me
and I smile.
This brings me great peace.
This brings me great joy.

"In the end, when we look at our lives,
the question will simply be:
Did I live fully? Did I love well?"

—*Jack Kornfield*

*Today I am taking the time to find everything
that is blocking me from joy and asking
God to help me release them.*

> "This is the day the Lord has made.
> Let us rejoice and be glad in it."
>
> —*The Bible, Psalm 118*

Living in this day, right now in this moment, is where we find our joy. But how many times do we hear people say things were better in the past? I remember my father saying, "Well, in my day children wouldn't act that way," and "You call this music! In my day . . ."

Just for the fun of it I looked up some quotes about the past, and it was fun to see how long people have been saying the same thing!

Cicero, who lived way back in 106–43 BC, said, "Oh, what times! What standards!" Catullus lived 87–54 BC: "Oh, this age! How tasteless and ill-bred it is!" Even further back, Socrates lived 470–399 BC and said, "Children today are tyrants. They contradict their parent, gobble their food, and tyrannize their teachers." And more recently, Matthew Arnold, who lived until 1888, said, "This strange disease of modern life, with its sick hurry, its divided aims."

Maybe our brains are wired to think like this. If so, when we do think yesterday was better, maybe now we can smile and see the absurdity of it, take a deep breath and bless this moment.

I am deeply grateful to be alive in this moment,
with all the gifts that come with this day.

> "If you understand—
> things are just as they are.
> If you don't understand—
> things are just as they are."
>
> —*Zen saying*

It's normal not to want or like to feel aches and pains that are natural as we grow older. Yet most of us do feel more aches and pains as we grow older.

It's normal to lose some of our energy as we grow older.

It's normal to forget some words and names as we grow older. Most of us do.

We only have two choices. One is to accept what is a normal part of our aging process and go on with our lives. And the other is to resist it. The first choice brings us a life of ease and contentment.

The second choice brings us stress. And since stress creates tension in our bodies, we feel more aches and pains, more loss of energy, and more loss of memory.

We all have this choice.

Ahhh, the peace and joy I feel when
I understand and accept things as they are!

my practice

"The mind can go in a thousand directions. But on this beautiful path, I walk in peace. With each step, gentle wind blows. With each step, flower blooms."

—*Thich Nhat Hanh*

Walking mindfully is a wonderful way to practice mindfulness and find joy. It is as simple as mindful breathing. We simply walk very slowly with full awareness, bringing our attention to our feet as they touch the ground or the rug. We're not walking to go anywhere. We are just enjoying each step. If thoughts come in, we notice them and return our awareness to our walking. Mindful walking is staying in *this* moment, enjoying *this* step. We can practice walking from the car to the house.

For longer walks we can be anywhere: at the beach, in our yard, on the street, or on a mountain trail. We can be aware of what we see around us. If the weather isn't conducive to going outside, we can walk in circles even in our living room or up and down a hallway.

Mindful walking is very helpful when uncomfortable feelings arise. Rather than speaking from a place of anger, take time to stop, breathe, and walk mindfully for a while. Stop the stories of anger, blame, and resentment, and come back to our hearts.

I am finding time to practice walking mindfully
today and enjoying the peace and joy.

"We all have dreams. But in order to
make dreams come into reality, it takes an
awful lot of determination, dedication,
self-discipline, and effort."

—*Jesse Owens*

While writing this book I was able to have a very large hands-on experience of aging when I had a total knee replacement. After very athletic younger years, severe arthritis had set in, and it was becoming more and more painful as time went on. In spite of it not being the best time to go through such an operation, I really had no choice. Afterward, a physical therapist came out to the house and helped me with the exercises that were horrendous and painful. She convinced me that if I didn't do them, I would not have full movement of my knee, so I did them.

My leg movements were so limited that I was able to see first-hand what it would be like to be handicapped or immobile. It has been a wonderful example of living with the determination and the courage to change the things I can.

*God gives me all the strength I need
to do what I have to do to improve
the quality of my life.*

with the help of
mindfulness

*I can begin each day making conscious contact
with the God of my understanding.*

good to know

The following is a wonderful exercise to help heal a relationship or seek forgiveness for something we have done in the past:

When we write with our nondominant hand, it brings us to a place deep inside that connects us to the right side of our brain, our creative, intuitive side. If we want to write to someone and make amends, for example, we would write with our nondominant hand, which will take us to a deep, intuitive place inside us.

We can also use this technique if we want to ask God a question. Say, for example, we would like to know what to do about a certain situation. We can write our question with our dominant hand and then answer it with our nondominant hand. We will often receive answers that will surprise us, because they come from our unconscious.

I am truly grateful to find so many ways
that help me heal and become free.

"Take care of your body.
It's the only place you have to live."

—*Jim Rohn*

As time passes, I've experienced a wonderful shift in the relationship with my body. During youth, the body was integral to identity, and I suffered when it didn't live up to the images of perfection advertised in fashion magazines. In middle age, it became a warrior, pushed to run marathons, work long hours, and otherwise be a servant to the whims of the mind. Today, as the hair grays, the wrinkles increase, and it noticeably slows down, I understand what a miracle it is to experience life through this human form, fleeting as it may be. I care for this impermanent body lovingly and humbly, with deep appreciation for the opportunity to have this vehicle to experience this wondrous world.

—*Angie Parrish*

in spite
of wrinkles

life love

*Today I am mindful to treat
my body with care and kindness,
knowing it is going to be with me
for as long as I live!*

my practice

I have finally come to see and accept
that I will never know it all,
that I will never do it all,
but what I do know
and what I have done
and will do
is enough.
It is good.
And I am grateful.

time for reflections

Did you ever stop and think about your thoughts
and where they come from?
Are they real?
How do they make you feel?
Have you noticed that when you have a thought,
your body responds with a feeling?
Take some time to be aware of your thoughts today.
Just notice a thought when it comes in.
Notice how long it stays.
Where does it go after you have it?
Is it a habitual thought?
Do you have it often?
Do you have similar thoughts over and over again?
Do your thoughts give you pain or bring you joy?
Can you stop the ones that bring you pain?
Can you change them to a thought that brings you joy?
When you see that you have the power to let go of
unpleasant thoughts, it's a wonderful feeling!
Why not let this be your mindfulness practice today!

"We can decide to live with joy,
or we can allow ourselves to live looking
back with bitterness."

—*Joan Chittister*

Have I forgiven everyone I have resented?
Have I forgiven myself for any mistakes I have made?
Am I carrying any guilt or shame?
Have I accepted everything that has happened in the past
and made peace with it so that I can
live in this moment with joy?

*Today I am taking time by myself in
mindful reflection to examine my past with honesty,
searching for any blocks I am still holding onto,
keeping me a prisoner. I pray that whatever
I find may be removed.*

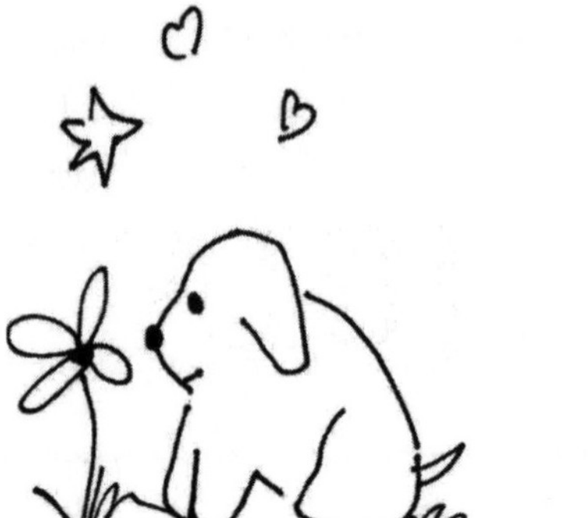

JULY

with the help of
mindfulness

*I can stop whenever I am tense, confused, angry,
or afraid, take three mindful breaths,
and feel peaceful.*

"Long live impermanence!
Without it a flower would never blossom,
a baby would never be able to walk or become
a teenager and grow into adulthood."

—*Thich Nhat Hahn*

One of the greatest causes of our suffering is our desire for the things we love to remain unchanged and the things we don't like to go away permanently. It is absolutely normal! Why in the world should we ever want a toothache or unpleasant people to stay in our lives? And if we could do something about it, wouldn't we make disease, war, poverty, and so on, disappear? Why in the world would we want to see our youthful faces change to wrinkles and our healthy bodies to be filled with aches and pains? It certainly goes without saying that we would never want the people we love to leave us and die.

Mindfulness helps us to let go of our resistance to the changes that are inevitable and to accept the present moment just as it is, whether the moment is pleasant, unpleasant, or neutral.

*I feel at peace today as I learn to
accept life on life's terms.*

Do I take time to just be quiet?
Do I take time to just be?
Perhaps to stop
and watch a butterfly
or look deeply inside
the very heart of a flower
or stop and be
with whatever
expresses itself
in
the
moment?

Today I am taking time to just be.

My breath is truly a miracle.
Whenever my mind brings me to fears of the unknown,
the future that isn't even here yet,
I can be mindful of my breath
and I can feel joy.
If I find myself worried about where I will live
and how I will get along when I get older,
I can return to my breath
and realize that I don't have answers
to a future that isn't here yet
and I can feel joy.
If I find myself worrying about
what I will do if my memory fails,
or if I run out of money
or if I get sick,
I can return to my breath
and realize that I don't have answers
to a future that isn't here yet
and I can feel joy.
All the ifs that haven't happened disappear . . .
As I breathe in and out in this moment
In this peaceful and perfect moment
where there is joy.

*I can keep my mind young by exercising it
every day with books, meditation, word games
and puzzles, physical exercise, healthy eating,
new activities, and good friends.*

"Due to our own wisdom,
we gradually stop strengthening habits
that only bring more pain
to the world."

—*Pema Chödrön*

Over the years we have accumulated individual, personal ways in which we react to life's circumstances. Unless we learn how to stop them, our habits take over and we don't even have to think about a response. We just respond from memory. Someone might have a different opinion than we have about something we strongly believe in. A person is mentioned in conversation whom you can't stand and you feel emotions rising effortlessly. A favorite ice cream is mentioned and your taste buds automatically respond. Our wants, likes, and dislikes become fixed over time.

As we become more and more mindful, we can catch the automatic reactions as they occur. We can stop, breathe, and not react.

*Today I am stopping how I habitually react
to things, and staying open to what I am
actually feeling in the moment.*

> "Whether we have ten days or ten years
> or thirty years, now, here, in this moment,
> we are learning that life is precious."
>
> —*Robert Raines*

My physical therapist recently shared with me how terrible she felt when she could no longer read her morning paper without glasses. She's 43 years old and it made her realize she was getting old and didn't like it. At different ages some of us need false teeth or tooth implants. I needed a knee replacement at 75 and felt very old and tired as I was recuperating. For some it is our hearing. For others, sagging skin, weak muscles, less energy, just to name a few changes that happen as we age.

When the knowledge that our time is limited on this earth hits us, it comes as a shock to some of us while others take it in our stride. We'll be much happier if we appreciate the miracle of our lives and count our blessings. Author Louise Hay, at 82, said, "I am a divine, infinite being—the age of my body has nothing to do with what I do or who I am."

> *I am so grateful for the years I have before me.*
> *I plan to live each day knowing it is a gift.*

"God gave you a gift of 86,400 seconds today.
Have you used one to say 'Thank you?'"

—*William A. Ward*

*It is amazing how quickly my negativity changes
into a positive mood when I think of just
one thing for which I am grateful.*

"It takes courage to grow up and
become who you really are."

—*e.e. cummings*

*It feels so good to finally come to this time
of my life when I can just be me!*

"Sooner or later we all discover that the important
moments in life are not the advertised ones, not the birth-
days, the graduations, the weddings, not the great goals
achieved. The real milestones are less prepossessing. They
come to the door of memory unannounced, stray dogs
that amble in, sniff around a bit and simply never leave.
Our lives are measured by these."

—*Susan B. Anthony*

"I look in the mirror through the eyes of the child that was
me." I see this crone, with eyes blue, faded by the years of
searching. The wrinkles of laughter and worry crinkle in thought
and delight as I squint at this image, but remember the child I
find myself still being.

My legs carry me stiffly albeit firmly; they creak, and age slows
their stubborn descent. I remember the hopscotch game, the race
to get the front seat of Dad's car, the dash down the beach to feel
the spray and splash of the Atlantic off Coney Island.

I hear the giggles of all the girls getting ready for the prom,
their hair shiny as they twirl and move to the unseen music of
the latest band. The boys in their sharply creased pants, shirts
starched with ties swaying, corsages in hand poised by the Plym-
outh, the Desoto, the Ford, doors ajar engines banging.

Mostly I see this couple, leaning over my crib. I see a man
grinning as he runs alongside a new bike and letting go when I
have succeeded. A hug, a kiss, and affection given freely. I see a
lazy hand drifting through my hair.

—*Carole Weissman*

*It's good to stop every once in a while and look back,
remembering the times that filled me with love and joy.*

> "It is our attachment to a particular self-image
> that makes us unhappy as we age."
>
> —*Ronald D. Siegel, Psy.D.*

If we can be mindful and accept that our looks are impermanent, it can be very helpful as we age. The more we try to
cling to looking good and feeling as fit as we did when we were
younger we will suffer. For, obviously, all this will change.

For years I took pride at having hardly any gray hair. Yet this
phenomenon had nothing to do with me or anything I had done
to make it happen. My mother's hair grayed in her late 60s. My
father, though mostly bald, had a mixture of black and grey hair
before he died at 93. It was my genes that decided my hair color.

One way to better accept our natural physical changes is to
picture what we looked like at 5 years old, at 10, at 15, and so
on, until you get to the age you are right now. Another way is to
examine the idea of our age being a part of the natural process
of nature. An acorn turns into an oak tree, a seed into a flower, a
puppy into a dog.

> *Today I celebrate who I am at the age I am*
> *and everything that brought me to*
> *this moment in my life!*

People often say that as they age they see more and more of their mother or father when they look in the mirror, and that it is depressing. If you can identify with this, why not try something different today. What we say to ourselves becomes a habit and what we think is what we feel. So obviously if you think "old" when you look in the mirror, you are going to feel "old."

Instead, smile and say "Good morning!" or "Hello!" or even "You are terrific!" or "You look great!"

It's hard to do this without smiling and you'll notice how warm and pleasant you will feel!

I feel younger and happier when I begin my day
with a smile and a positive greeting.

mindful techniques

"There are many stages in mental development, but as soon as we are able to maintain the mind in a calm state, at that very moment there is joy and peace. This is reflected in the body becoming relaxed, and then the mind becomes more relaxed. As the mind calms down, the hidden enlightened qualities emerge more and more."

—*Venerable Khenpo Tsewang Dongyal Rinpoche*

Spend some time each day focusing on your breath coming in and going out or focusing on counting each breath from 1 to 5, and then do it over again until you feel calm. Remain in that calm state called "calm abiding." You're no longer attached to thoughts or feelings. You see them come in and pass away. You feel them but you are not attached to them. They are just there.

All the better if you can have a smile on your face when you are practicing. It will add to the calm and joy you feel. Spend some time each day on this or another form of mindfulness and watch how it changes your life.

My life is getting better and better. I am happier and filled with peace as I practice mindfulness every day.

mindful peace

"Old people don't get crabby.
Crabby people get old."

—Steve Otto

When I was younger I remember observing some old people who were cranky and impatient and stuck in their ways and thinking that I never wanted to turn out like them. I was determined that I would be different. I would be pleasant and uncomplaining.

I discovered God through a 12-step program in my thirties and mindfulness meditation in my forties. Both gave me the tools to live a positive life as they led me in the direction of compassion and love for myself and others. I certainly have cranky, unpleasant moods, and there are times when I just don't feel pleasant, but these times are few and far between.

These two parallel paths actually teach me that I have a choice. If I feel irritable, impatient, or cranky, I can turn my day over to God. I can stop, ask for help, breathe mindfully a few times, and relax. I can breathe in peace and breathe out tension. I can wait before responding in a negative or unpleasant way. I can choose to be the person I want to be.

*I am so grateful I have found a path that guides me
in a meaningful, positive, and loving life.*

time for reflections

If I knew I had only one day, one month, one year, five years to live,
what would I do with my time?
With whom would I spend it?
Where would I go?
Where would I turn to get strength to get through this?

higher
power

"I could not, at any age, be content to take
my place in a corner by the fireside
and simply look on."

—*Eleanor Roosevelt*

S ome of us think about the retirement years and look forward
to playing golf or doing other things that make us happy.
Others vow to never retire—they say they love what they do and
want to keep doing it for as long as they can. Some plan a bit of
both, doing what they enjoy and perhaps volunteering and doing
service work in some way.

And some people give this no thought at all and just drift
along into retirement years doing less and less and soon having
no ambition to do anything at all.

It is important that we give this time in our lives a great deal
of thought so the years won't just slip by and we will continue to
find meaning in our lives.

*I pray that I may appreciate the miracle of
my life and live it fully every day.*

good to know

Every time we have a thought our brain releases chemicals. We become aware of what we are thinking when an electric transmission goes across our brain. If we have a negative or angry thought, negative chemicals make us feel bad. If we have a positive, happy thought our brain releases positive chemicals and we feel good. Our bodies react to all our thoughts.

Negative, stressful thoughts actually harm our bodies by causing us to become tense. Our heart rate increases and a strain is placed on many other organs. Until we learn how to become aware of what we are thinking, our thoughts respond to what is going on in our lives in a very habitual way.

Mindfulness teaches us to be aware of what we are thinking. As a thought comes in, we can recognize it, bring our awareness to it. And once aware, we can choose to change our thought if we want and thus change how we feel.

I am so grateful I no longer am a robot,
reacting to thoughts without knowing it. I can
change my thoughts and therefore change how
I feel and be in charge of my life today.

"Meditation helps us to relinquish old, painful habits. . . .
To live in a way that enables us to respect ourselves."
—*Sharon Salzberg*

We have ways of thinking that we accept and believe. For example, we might have a thought such as *I'm not good in social situations,* or *I'll never have enough money to retire.* With mindfulness we can learn to question these thoughts.

Author Byron Katie developed a simple technique called "The Work," which she uses to question whether our thoughts are true. She suggests we ask ourselves the following questions when something is bothering us.

1. Is it true?
2. Can you absolutely know that it's true?
3. How do you react, what happens, when you believe that thought?
4. Who would you be without the thought?

This is a wonderful practice to help us stop automatically thinking something is true just because we think it.

I choose to no longer accept any negative thoughts. I now question any thought that doesn't make me feel good and this gives me great joy!

"Everything changes—but some things
change more slowly."

—Janice Clark

It's comforting to be reminded that change, like wrinkles, is inevitable.

And how good it is that we are gifted with recall. Had God not redirected my willful efforts a few decades ago, I'd not be here enjoying this opportunity to share with others. I had a far different journey in mind.

The most difficult part of change is that it often comes after we have settled into a routine that pleases us and we don't like the signs of change that we see on the horizon. However, on the other side of change we will find a deeper level of awareness, love, and certainty about the journey on which we find ourselves. That's the promise we have been made by the God of our understanding.

The joy in growing older, I think, is that we have the opportunity to revisit the past in fond memories. Then we can strengthen our trust that the present and the future will give us more fond memories to be resurrected when the need for them arrives.

Wrinkles never go away. In much the same way, change never ends. Let's honor each one. They are special and specific to who we are.

—Karen Casey

Change is a gift. We simply didn't know we had been waiting for it.

"To meditate does not mean to fight with a problem.
To meditate means to observe. Your smile proves it.
It proves that you are being gentle with yourself,
that the sun of awareness is shining in you, that you
have control of your situation. You are yourself,
and you have acquired some peace."

—*Thich Nhat Hanh*

A ging joyfully may be tremendously affected by various illnesses which seem to be alleviated only by entering into the world of peace and meditation. Dwelling on unpleasant or negative personal issues does nothing but exacerbate them. However, I have found that meditation and intense remembrance of peaceful and joyful moments are my way to maintain peace, joy, and comfort in my life.

These times of peace and solitude enable me to face the many issues which are included in the unalterable physical and mental changes that come with aging.

—*Elaine Emery*

*Today I watch all the physical and
mental changes age has brought on. It
will stop bothering me as I enter the
world of peace and meditation.*

I
feel
so
free
when I
let go
of
anything that
is happening in
my life
that is
negative
and feel the
gratitude
for what is good
and positive.

good to know

"When you bring your attention to
the things you are grateful for in your life,
your brain actually works better."

—*Daniel Amen*

In a test examining gratitude and appreciation, a woman had her brain scanned after 30 minutes of meditating on all the things she was thankful for in her life. Then she was scanned a few days later after focusing on all the major fears for her life. When she was grateful, her temporal lobe looked healthy. When she focused on fearful thoughts, her temporal lobe became much less active.

With the practice of mindfulness we can be more aware of our thoughts. When we find that our moods are down or blue or we are aware we are fearful, we can ask ourselves what we are thinking that is creating these feelings. And we can change it to something for which we are grateful.

*It's wonderful to know that I can bring
more joy in my life when I practice
gratitude every day.*

"If the only prayer you ever say in
your entire life is thank you,
it will be enough."

—*Meister Eckhart*

D r. Daniel Amen found that when depressed patients daily wrote five things for which they were grateful, they actually needed less antidepressant medication. Others studies have shown that people who express gratitude on a regular basis are healthier, more optimistic, make more progress toward their goals, have a greater sense of well-being, and are more helpful to others.

Could it possibly be that easy? Why not start today and practice this for a week or a month and see if you feel different from when you began.

*I love how I feel when I start
my day with gratitude!*

> "It's no longer necessary to wait for
> people or situations to change in order to
> experience peace and harmony."
>
> —*Byron Katie*

How many times have you said, "If only he or she would change or do this or do that for me, then I would be happy"? Or you might think, "If only I felt better or had more energy or more money or had this or that then I would be content."

Let's practice today letting all the "if onlys" go. Know that we don't need anything else to be happy. We can be happy in this moment, right now, by simply accepting what is. Once we let go of our "if onlys" we are free to live in this moment, just as it is. This doesn't mean we don't work for goals or want to improve our lives if we can. It means that we don't need our lives to be better for us to be happy. This is how and where we find joy.

I pray today to accept my life as it is,
finding joy in what I have.

No matter what our age, if we are mindful, open, honest and willing, we can still discover new truths about us.

When we look deeply, we can peel away layers and layers of false self and discover the magnificent person we truly are.

I pray for the willingness and honesty to
continue to discover the wonderful
human being I really am.

I Ain't Much, Baby—But I'm All I Got!

—Title of a book by Jess Lair

Many years ago I read this book by Jess Lair, and there was one concept that has stayed with me ever since. He wrote about a time when he was in the hospital recovering from a heart attack when he realized that he felt good with certain people in his life. He made the decision to hang out only with people who made him feel ten feet tall! I remember thinking "How obvious! Of course!"

Jess wrote "I came to feel that was the most loving thing I could do for anyone—tell them how it was with me and share my imperfections with them. When I did this, most people came back at me with what was deep within them. This was love coming to me. And the more I had coming to me, the more I had to give away."

We don't need to stay with people who put us down, who criticize us, who think they know how we should live our lives. We feel good with people who make us feel ten feet tall! People who respect us. People who don't try to change us but accept us as we are.

Today my friends are people who make
me feel ten feet tall and I do
the same for them!

my practice

For so many years
I took life for granted.
I rushed from day to day,
doing what is in front of me,
not taking time to appreciate
what was around me.
Now, at this time of my life,
I am learning to slow down
and be more mindful
of the wonderful gift
that is
life.

"Modern neuroscience tells us that our past reactions are engraved onto synapses that send messages from one neuron to another, making them more likely to send the same message in the future.... Mindfulness gives us the option to choose a healthier response."

—*Jack Kornfield*

It is so exciting to discover that so many of our reactions are just habits! While still in high school, I raised my hand to answer a question the teacher had asked the class. I was wrong! I still remember waves of embarrassment pouring over me and I vowed I would never volunteer to speak in public again.

Years later, with the publication of my first book, *The Journey Within: A Spiritual Path to Recovery,* my publisher asked me to speak at a conference. I had the immediate reaction I had as a teenager, waves and waves of fear came over me and I said no. In spite of my insistence not to speak, he put me on the agenda. I was petrified, but with the help of positive affirmations and practice, I eventually got over my fear and actually enjoy public speaking.

The next chance you get, stop, breathe, and look deeply into the source of your fear. You can gradually change your reactions by realizing that your fear comes from something a long time ago and has nothing to do with the present moment. By allowing yourself to have new experiences your habitual fear will disappear.

I can let go of my fears of the past just by realizing
their source is in my past and has nothing
to do with the present moment.

"I am only one, but I am one.
I cannot do everything, but I can do something.
And I will not let what I cannot do
interfere with what I can do."

—*Edward Everett Hale*

The phrase "sedentary agitation" recently popped into my life and struck a chord deep within my heart. It means being regularly upset by all you see but not getting up and doing anything about it. Often, as we get older, we are less apt to speak up, to reach out. To me, "sedentary agitation" is a call to action. The first step is to nurture the seeds of love we each have within us, compassionately accepting that we all have imperfections, struggles, self-doubt. By learning to love ourselves, we can ground ourselves in the bedrock of our inherent basic goodness. We will see the world, not through the veil of fear in our heads, but from our hearts, with clarity and openness—like wiping the dust of confusion from the mirror reflecting who we really are. Bravery and compassion will blossom as we realize we all can stand tall in our own way, even if the deck seems stacked against us. We can simultaneously look within and reach out—right where we live. We can be the change. We can ask ourselves one simple question: What am *I* doing to make the world a better place?

—*Liam Phillips Lindsay*

*I am committed to do something today to make
the world a better place for someone.*

"Sometimes the most important thing
in a whole day is the rest we take between two
deep breaths, or the turning inwards in
prayer for five short minutes."

—Etty Hillesum

In times of irritation or upset,

fear or frustration,

in short,

any time

when we are not feeling peaceful . . .

simply stop.

Feel your breath coming in and going out.

Do this a few times

And notice the space between your breaths.

Simply be aware of that space

and then notice

the change in how you are feeling now

from how you were feeling a few minutes ago.

Our breath is a gift.

All we have to do is

notice it.

> "... We need to constantly investigate
> the true nature of things. This constant investigation
> will eliminate deluded thoughts and lead to the
> understanding of the true nature of the mind."
>
> —*Dilgo Khyentse Rinpoche*

O ur thoughts can scare us by telling us all the things we have to fear as we grow old. What if we are alone? What if we won't have enough money? What if we can't take care of ourselves? What if we are sick?

By practicing mindfulness, we can see that these are just thoughts. Nothing remains but our memory of them. Of course, you can bring them back by choice. And they can come back by habit, but they are only words that create fear. They have absolutely no truth.

By practicing mindfulness, we can see these words for what they are, just words. We can stop and even smile. We can say to ourselves, "These are just words."

We can breathe in and out three times and watch them disappear. We can be aware that the future is not here, and that we have no idea in this moment what we will be like 2, 5, 10, 20 years from now. We can bring our awareness to the reality that we are okay right now. And if any of these thoughts were real, we would still be okay and find a way to live with their reality.

I am so grateful that I am learning to understand that my thoughts are not my reality and no matter what is going on in the present moment, I am okay.

AUGUST

did you know?

When I was younger I was a tomboy. I loved sports and was active in everything from tennis, basketball, and softball to horseback riding. Being very competitive, I played on all the teams they had for girls' sports in grammar school and high school. My activities began to drop off by the time I reached college, and in the years that followed my energies went more to my family and my creative side, rather than to sports.

I thought that exercise was boring and never wanted to participate in gym. When I was much older I knew I had to do something about becoming more active but still dreaded joining a gym. But boring or not, exercise is so important as we grow older.

Studies show that when the body is active, it signals the brain to be ready to learn and grow. Active adults have better overall blood supply to their brains and they experience fewer or smaller strokes so common with age. Exercise supports brain health, longevity, and immunological functions. Studies show that it appears to trigger neuroplastic changes in the brain that enhance attention, energy, and learning.

Listening to music or to a talk on an MP3 player while exercising can help make the time pass more quickly. Many gyms have a TV setup with their exercise machines. Whatever it takes, know that you are helping yourself mentally, physically, and even spiritually.

I pray for the discipline to make exercise
a regular part of my life.

"Yesterday is ashes. Tomorrow is green wood.
Only today does the fire burn brightly."

—*Eskimo saying*

One day in August, while living on Cape Cod, I noticed that the grass hadn't been cut in weeks. And it didn't need it yet. There had been plenty of rain. That couldn't be the reason. And the sun had been out, too. I looked around and noticed that the weeds were not nearly as overwhelming as they had been just a few weeks earlier. Had they slowed down, too, in their growth? Why, just a few weeks ago I couldn't keep up with them.

That's similar to where I am in my life right now, I thought. I had just finished a large project. No energy for new growth. Tired. No new blossoms or branches. Was I slowing down my growth, too? Was I getting ready to change my leaves and let them fall off, to rest, to dig in and hibernate until the spring, when I would have more energy to blossom again? Or was I just getting old?

I didn't have the answer to this. I knew life would just have to unfold, a day at a time, and I would know the answers when I needed them.

*It is very transforming to know that I do not
need to have all the answers to my life right now.
I can practice patience and mindfulness and
enjoy each moment one breath at a time.*

We age.
Bending is painful
Skin folds on itself
and self-recognition is a surprise party every morning.

Disease knocks unwelcome
loss, fatigue, pain, loneliness arrive

Yet there is wisdom,
joy, love awareness and
beauty, sweetness
laughter, renewal
we let go!

We have family, friends, sons and daughters
we nurtured, witness evolve into
creatures of incredible delights
a renewable daily gift,
our bounty of love growing
daily (never imaginable in our youth)

We have learned
love always, love eternal
alive in
us
Wrinkles? Who cares!

—*Bonny Van de Kamp*

*goodbye stress
hello joy*

Anyone who stops learning is old,
whether at twenty or eighty.
Anyone who keeps learning stays young.

It has been proven by many studies over the years that mental stress leads to faster aging and that it's not always outside stressors that are the most important, but our responses to those stressors. It has also been proven that relaxation—a state of calm, peace, and stillness—can regenerate and renew your tissues and organs. Scientists have even shown how meditation makes the brain bigger and better. They said that by learning to create positive brain states through deep relaxation or meditation, you can:

- Reduce inflammation
- Help regenerate your organs and cells by activating stem cells
- Increase your heart rate variability
- Thicken your brain (which normally shrinks with aging)
- Boost immune function
- Modulate your nervous system
- Reduce depression and stress
- Improve your quality of life

*It's exciting to know that my daily meditation practice is keeping
my brain and body healthy and slowing down my aging.*

It's incredible how
much younger
and lighter
I
feel
when I
let go
of
all thoughts of
the past
and the
future
and stay
mindful
in the
present moment.

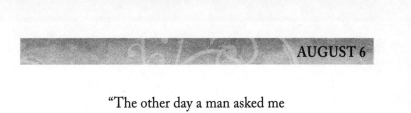

"The other day a man asked me
what I thought was the best time of life.
'Why,' I answered without a thought, 'now.'"

—*David Grayson*

*living in the
"now"*

Becoming Aware of Awareness

A good way to practice mindfulness, which is really being aware
in the present moment, is to
   sit quietly and simply and
      be aware of your breath.
   After a few moments, bring your awareness
      to your breath in your body.
      Feel your chest rising and falling.
      Your stomach filling and emptying.
   Bring your awareness down through your hips and buttocks
      Your thighs and your knees
      Your legs
      ankles
      toes.
   And then bring your awareness
      back to your breath.
   Are you aware that tension has left your body?
      Your mind?
   Are you aware that you are aware?
   Can you simply sit and be aware that you are aware?
   Can you smile while all this is happening?
   Can you feel peace?
   Can you feel joy?

"Because of mindfulness, we see our desire, and our aggression, our jealousy and our ignorance. We don't act on them; we just see them. Without mindfulness, we don't see them and they proliferate."

—*Pema Chödrön*

Mindfulness gives us the ability to examine ourselves honestly. The more we get to know ourselves and watch how we react to life, we learn that our thoughts give us the most trouble. Author Judith Viorst writes that the greatest stresses of life are likely to occur in our later years. The mean may become meaner, the fearful may get more afraid, and the apathetic may sink into near-paralysis. With mindfulness, see that when we have fearful thoughts, we can change them. When we watch the stories we create, we can see when they are carrying us off into anger and resentments or predictions of bad things to come. If we see we are acting mean we can let those thoughts go. We can change what we think and learn to live more in the present moment. We can pray and develop more trust in the God of our understanding.

We can learn that we don't have to be miserable, mean, or fearful. We can grow older feeling good about ourselves. We can find joy in the later years of our lives.

There is great power in knowing that I am in charge of my thoughts. How I choose to feel as I age is up to me and I choose to live a life of love and compassion and joy.

"You are invited to live more consciously,
to get off auto pilot and cruise control. To try
new things to find out who you really
are in this moment and time."

—*James Hollis, Ph.D.*

I have a good friend in her 60s who has just moved to Colorado for a new job because she feels "called on" to work in a hospice. Two other good friends, also in their late 60s, spent two years in Thailand for the Peace Corps because they, too, felt "called on" to serve in this way. Sometimes the "call" comes as a strong pull, inspiring us to move in a certain direction. Other times an opportunity appears and we "know" it is what we are supposed to do.

What if you hear it or feel it? Be patient. Be quiet. Ask your inner guide. Pray to the God of your understanding for your answer. If you are willing and sincere it will come. You don't have to move to Colorado or Thailand. Just as important, you might see if a neighbor needs a ride to the store or the dentist. Perhaps it's offering to donate blood.

*It feels so good to spend
some of my time helping others.
I find great joy in this service.*

"If you want to walk faster, you walk alone.
If you want to walk farther,
you walk together."

—*African saying*

*I can use all I have learned
to help someone else.*

"Those who bring sunshine to the lives of others
cannot keep it from themselves."

—*James Matthew Barrie*

Many years ago, when I was newly sober, I was very depressed and very needy. I went up to a beautiful place in New Hampshire where the St. Frances prayer was painted on a very large sign. Some of the words were:

Lord, make me an instrument of your peace . . .
grant that I may not so much seek to be consoled as to console;
to be understood as to understand;
to be loved as to love.

And I thought, I need to be consoled. I need to be understood. I need to be loved. I can't do this for anyone else.

Recently I made a greeting card for a friend's celebration, and as I inserted a little inspirational book I had written, I felt a feeling of great joy. What a dramatic change over the years! It was wonderful to remember where I was then and where I am now. It is certainly not just because of mindfulness, although that is part of it. I have been on a spiritual journey for many years so that I no longer am the needy, self-centered person I once was.

*I am so grateful that I no longer think of just
myself and can feel great joy in being
other-centered and generous.*

After a speech one day, Zig Ziglar was
approached by someone in the audience who said:
"Zig, it was a great speech, but motivation doesn't last.
Zig said, "Bathing doesn't either.
That's why I recommend it daily!"

As we learn to practice mindfulness, it takes time to be aware of the present moment and the thoughts we are having. That is why we practice every day. We sit in morning meditation a suggested minimum of twenty minutes and then practice bringing this same attention to the rest of our day.

We have spent all our previous years being unaware that we have any control over our thoughts. Our minds have gone to the past and the present. There's a well-known example of what is called "monkey mind" that describes our minds as being like monkeys, jumping from branch to branch, doing whatever they want to do. In mindfulness, we learn to tame the monkey mind.

So please be patient. If you find that your mind has been in the past or the future—know that you are successful at being mindful because you did notice it! And once you do, you can just come back to the present moment. Meditation teacher Thich Nhat Hanh tells us that it is not how many times we went away from our breathing but how many times we notice it and come back to the present moment, this breath.

I am developing a daily practice of sitting mindfully
each morning, quietly watching my breath, calming my mind,
and connecting with a power greater than myself. It feels so
transforming to then bring this practice to the rest of my day.

"The most beautiful people we have known are those
who have known defeat, known suffering, known struggle,
known loss, and have found their way out of the depths.
Beautiful people do not just happen."

—*Elisabeth Kübler-Ross*

It would be a rare person who has not experienced some loss, some pain in life. Some of us have certainly had more than others. Grief and joy, victory and defeats fall into the natural cycle of life as do hurricanes and rainbows, summer and winter.

Some of us have become passionate about not letting others suffer as we have and become inspired to help others. MADD, Mothers Against Drunk Driving, for example, was started by a woman who lost her daughter when she was hit by a drunk driver. Alcoholics Anonymous was founded by two men who taught others how they finally stayed sober after years of painful, uncontrollable drinking.

You might consider sharing how you healed from any struggle you have been through or how you turned around a defeat to victory. We have so much to offer others as a power of example through our own life experience, and as we share these strengths we continue to grow and heal.

It feels so good to be able to turn around my
loss into something that can help others.

"Although we cannot reverse our chronological age, we can reverse the more important measures of our biological and psychological age—and by doing so we can regain the physical and emotional vitality we had in the past."

—*Deepak Chopra, M.D.*

A helpful way of looking at our age is to divide it into three categories: chronological age, biological age, and psychological age—our subjective experience of how old we are.

There are people who are 70 who feel like 50 and thus act it, and there are people who are 50 who feel like 70 and act it. Which would you rather be?

Deepak Chopra, M.D., says we can improve our psychological age by learning to relax and enjoy life. He suggests there are many factors which will help us including diet, exercise, and changing our perceptions. A study by Harvard psychologist Ellen Langer took a group of men in their 70s and 80s and encouraged them to think and behave as if they were 20 years younger. After only 5 days, a number of physical changes associated with age reversed in these men. Their hearing and vision improved, they performed better on tests of manual dexterity, and they had improved joint mobility.

Our thoughts can actually change our bodies. For example, when we relax instead of becoming tense, our immune system becomes stronger. When we notice our thoughts with the help of mindfulness, we can change our thoughts to ones that help us relax.

As I am learning to become more and more mindful of my thoughts I am experiencing the excitement of feeling younger and I have much more joy in my life.

"If you have one eye on yesterday, and one eye on
tomorrow, you're going to be cockeyed today."

—*Author unknown*

Regardless of our age, we really only have today . . . this moment.
With the practice of mindfulness, I can catch myself quicker
when I worry about the future or waste precious time and energy
reliving the past. If I can remember to engage in a simple task
(such as making the bed or sorting papers at work) and say softly
out loud to myself each action that I'm taking, it forces me to
stay right in the now. Therefore, it's almost impossible to obsess
about the future while describing the process of making up the
bed. For example, "Now I'm pulling the fitted sheet to the corner
of the mattress; now I'm shaking out the top flat sheet; now I'm
smoothing it out and getting it centered; and now I'm tucking
in the corners of the flat sheet under the mattress . . ." and so on.
When I can do this, it helps my mind be "where my feet are" and
not somewhere else. And, inevitably, if I stop and examine my situation, I find that I have everything I really need in this moment.

—*Christopher Bolgiano*

*Just being in the present moment and
doing simple things such as making the bed
or sipping tea can give me great joy.*

"... People who only work out at the gym
are not as smart as people who go to the gym and
work out at the library. At every age, exercise
helps keep the brain healthy."

—*Daniel Amen*

*I can picture new brain cells growing
as I exercise my body and my brain today!
It feels so good to be taking
care of myself!*

"I don't want my wrinkles taken away—
I don't want to look like everyone else."

—Jane Fonda

I'm running out of time to say, "I'm 60-something!" as the "the big birthday" looms ever nearer. Living in a social environment that worships youth, I don't fit in. We see a standard look for people who are young, slim, strong, and on top of things. I am none of these, but does that mean I am not what I should be?

Nothing is where it used to be as skin and muscles move south. I look in the mirror: are these wrinkles or wisdom lines? Is this white hair a crown of glory? How is it that what is on the outside does not reflect what I know on the inside? How thankful I am to know that Spirit is eternal. Although I could be discriminated against for being female, old, differently-abled, and Christian, She holds me in the hand of love, joy, hope, and peace. I have chosen to call myself "differently-abled" rather than dis-abled. Although my legs no longer run like a deer, I am pressing on toward my Higher Calling, I continue to see with eyes of Faith and let go of inconsequential things, holding on always to hope. And at times when the mountain seems too high, I choose joy; that is my strength.

—Deacon Bonnie Moore

*It feels so good to have lived, seen, smelled, touched,
felt pain, loved, and rejoiced. I know that Spirit has set
my course and will see me through on a path of
Peace and I embrace the wisdom wrinkles!*

What face do you display as you age?
A face of suffering?
Triumphs?
Hopes?
Joys?
Or a mixture of all? Or nothing?
What part of you do you let other people see?
What are you hiding?
What have you made peace with?
What are you hanging on to?
What keeps you from being fully you?

"There is only one journey. Going inside yourself."
—*Rainer Maria Rilke*

We often hear and read that mediation brings you to your true self. But what does this exactly mean? What are we looking for? Where, even, is within? Is there such a place?

All this takes time to sort out in quiet and in solitude. When we take the time in mindfulness to quiet our mind, to stop our thoughts from going to the past and the future, and simply be here in the present moment, we can discover who we really are. Not who others want us to be and not who we think we should be but who we really are. When we make meditation a daily part of our lives, all this will be revealed.

When we let go of what the world tells us we should be, we find our own wants and needs, we find our own virtue and goodness. We might find our inner child who has been hurt and needs our healing and love. We might find sadness at our unfulfilled dreams. We can discover the fears that have kept us from being who we truly are. We can learn to trust our intuition, our inner knowing. We can love ourselves for who we really are and find that place of peace and joy within that has always been there, but was buried under our fears and disappointments and mistakes.

Today I am taking quiet time alone to find the very special person deep within me whom I can love and nurture and accept, just as I am, and this brings me great joy.

It's peaceful when I
stop
whatever I am doing
a few times
each day
and simply
breathe

.

.

feel my breath
as it is going in
and going out
and

.

.

I
smile

It Feels So Good to Know

I am at choice today.
Some part of my life is always at choice.
I can hold on to thoughts
that fill me with
bitterness and resentment
or I can let go
and breathe
and think thoughts of
forgiveness and
compassion and
love

"I am an old man and have known a great many
troubles, but most of them never happened."

—*Mark Twain*

Over the years we accumulate habits, and until we stop and do some
mindful self-searching, we don't even realize that we can change.

Worrying is a good example. I have spoken to many people who
worry all the time. "Why, of course I worry," they say. "It's my children
who are going through so much," or "How am I going to pay my bills?"
and so on. Worry is such a normal part of their lives that they don't even
know another way. Worry keeps us from inner peace and contentment
and drags our spirits down. If you identify with any of this you might
want to consider giving it up and enjoying the rest of your life with
more freedom.

How can we let go of worry? It takes time and practice. Each time
you find yourself worrying, take a conscious, mindful breath.

Feel it. Feel your breath as it goes in and out from your nose. Feel
your chest as it rises and falls.

Find that space between the in breath and the out breath when
nothing is happening, that pause between breaths.

You'll know the absence of worry in that moment. Even for a brief
time you will experience it.

Your mind will feel free and light.

You will feel free and light.

This won't take worrying away completely, but in time worrying will
be less of a burden. You are learning to use conscious, mindful breathing to let go.

It feels so good to let go of the worrying that
has been blocking me from being free.

good to know

Modern science tells us that out past reactions are engraved into the synapses of our brain that send messages from one neuron to the other, making them more likely to send the same message in the future. For example, if we were bitten by a dog when we were young, every time our ears hear the sound of a dog barking, our brain reacts the same way it did when we were younger and sends a signal of fear to our bodies.

Mindfulness allows us to be aware that this reaction is a saved message from our past that has been playing over and over again, and over time we can let it go and respond from the present moment.

It feels so good to be free of old reactions
and to live in the present moment.

It's incredible how
much younger
and lighter
I
feel
when I
turn my
life
over
to the
God
of my
understanding

"When we live without meaning,
we suffer the greatest illness of all."

—*James Hollis, Ph.D.*

Our desire for comfort, security, predictability, love, and material things can keep us from stretching ourselves, exploring who we really are, and finding out the deeper more important meaning and purpose of our lives. We might find ourselves depressed and don't know why. Something is missing and we don't know what.

With mindfulness we can look deeply and explore what is happening on the inside. We can discover what is appropriate now at our particular age to live a more meaningful life. We can examine habits we have developed over the years and find the ones that have held us back from living a mindful life.

I am so grateful for the practice of mindfulness that illuminates the dark places of my life and helps me discover what I can do to live a richer, fuller life.

*Today I am looking deeply into myself and letting
my soul guide me to my next step.*

> "An open heart holds the space
> for all humanity because it knows and
> loves its own humanity."
>
> —*Lynne Kloss*

The waves of emotion inside me are calmer now at
    58 than when I was 50 or 8.
My suggestions to others carry less judgment and criticism.
And my hips scream at me when I sit for too long.

I am very grateful for having been born human.
I am beginning to feel like a dandelion gone to seed.
I am present for whatever blows my way.

I aspire to breathe deeply and mindfully as if each breath
    is my last.
I aspire to live each moment with the openness and
    curiosity of a five-year-old.
I aspire to love, knowing we all share the
    same heart.

—*Nancy Natilson*

It
feels
so good to
sit
and
breathe
and watch
my mind
do what
it wants to do
until eventually
it does
what I want
it to do

.

.

.

rest
in the present moment

"Do not have your concert first
and tune your instruments afterwards.
Begin the day with God."

—James Hudson Taylor

I have been meditating for over 30 years. In fact, the only two times I left the house before meditating was when catching an early flight, and then I meditated in the car while someone else was driving. Most of the time I read something inspirational first. Then I meditate and pray. If I am running late, I give up the reading, but never the meditation and prayer.

Many people ask why morning is the best time to meditate. I explain my reasoning with the example of a heater in a cold room. If you turn on the heater in the morning, you'll have a warm room all day. If you wait until noon, you'll be cold in the morning. And if you wait until evening, you will be cold all day!

Meditating makes me aware of my breath, aware of the moment, and by meditating in the morning, I am more mindful during my entire day. Meditating is a time for me to make a conscious contact with God and I want to have God in my life all day.

*I look forward to beginning each morning
with mindful meditation the simple act that
brings me peace throughout the day.*

mindful techniques

Today I am reflecting on my breath.
I'm bringing my full awareness to my breath.
I'm acting as if I never really noticed my breath before.
Is it warm or cold?
Rough or smooth?
Deep or shallow?
Can I feel it on the skin on the
tip of my nose?
Or above my lip?
How deep inside
can I feel my breath?
Can I feel it more on one side
than the other?
The right or the left?
Resting in nothing else but the
awareness
of my breath
quiets my mind and
brings me great peace.
It brings me great joy.

good to know

On the Japanese Island of Okinawa,
people eat about 30 percent fewer calories than
their compatriots elsewhere in Japan.
Okinawa has almost 40 times as many centenarians
per capita as the rest of the country.

There is so much information coming out every day about how the food we eat affects our health. The more mindful we stay about our diet, the healthier we will remain as we grow older. We might not live to be 100 years old, but we will feel much better whatever age we are.

*It feels so good to know that I can do
something positive for my health by being
mindful of the food that I eat.*

SEPTEMBER

"There is a criterion by which you can
judge whether the thoughts you are thinking and
the things you are doing are right for you.
The criterion is:
Have they brought you inner peace?"

—*Peace Pilgrim*

*It feels so joyful to be filling my life with
thoughts of peace, love, compassion, forgiveness,
generosity, and acceptance.*

Today's Mindful Reflection

"Mindfulness meditation, in its pure and classic sense,
is about finding your true self. It is about waking up to the
true nature of the present moment. As you look deeply
into yourself and other beings in the world, you will have
the opportunity to free yourself from the concepts that
you have about everything, including who you are."

—*Andrew Weiss*

A m I willing to look deeply into the concepts I have carried for years and examine them?

Am I willing to let go of the concepts I have carried for years and be open to look at everything in a new light without judgment?

Am I willing to live in this moment only, free from the past experiences that have influenced my concepts and judgments?

Am I willing to give up all the concepts I have believed because others have said they are true and look at my life with my eyes only?

*It is so freeing to be
willing to let go of all the
concepts I have been carrying
with me and discover who
I am in this very moment.*

"How pleasant is the day when we give up
trying to be young—or slender!"

—*William James*

We're bombarded with messages from the television, news-paper, and Internet that younger is prettier, more hand-some, better, more popular, more attractive. We're bombarded with merchandise, recipes, and advice to keep us young or return us to looking and feeling youthful. This is a multimillion-dollar industry, and we struggle to stay young.

We dye our hair, wear wigs and toupees, work out at the gym, go on diets, copy the clothes that superstars wear, and completely lose our individual identity trying to be someone else. Not that the gym and diets are wrong. Naturally, they're important in staying healthy. But when we do them to look younger, that's when we get in trouble.

Why is it so hard to just be ourselves sometimes?

*Today I am praying for the courage and
acceptance to be myself completely and to know
that I am terrific just the way I am!*

"The thing that upsets people is not
what happens but what they think it means."
—*Greek philosopher Epictetus*

There are many ways to change our interpretation of what our thoughts mean, and unless we find a way that works for us, our thoughts lead us into depression. Dr. Andrew Weil tells us that depression is often rooted in habitual thoughts of worthlessness and isolation, and that as we age, we become more susceptible to this kind of thinking.

Cognitive behavioral therapy is one way to let go of this type of thinking. We have to learn to stop judging everything as good or bad and learn that we can change the way we think.

The Buddha taught we suffer from unhappiness when we judge every experience as either pleasant, unpleasant, or neutral, and we try to hold on to the pleasant experiences while pushing away the unpleasant. He taught that with mindfulness we can observe the process of thought without getting attached to it. We can simply watch our thoughts and let them go.

Scientists have also learned within the last 40 years that meditation can be as powerful as medication for reversing depression. They both stimulate the feel-good chemical serotonin in our brains. As we become mindful of thoughts of worthlessness or fear, by meditating and learning to change our thoughts from fear to faith or gratitude or self-love, anything positive, we can turn depression around to good feelings.

I am so grateful that the simple habit of mindfulness
can help me to feel good about myself as I grow older,
and to live a happier, more joyful life.

"The fact that I can plant a seed and it becomes a flower,
share a bit of knowledge and it becomes another's,
smile at someone and receive a smile in return,
are to me continual spiritual exercises."

—*Leo Buscaglia*

Recently, on a trip to Alaska, I connected for just a few minutes with an Inuit Eskimo named O'Jack. Our encounter was so brief, and yet in the few minutes that we spoke there was a spiritual connection that spanned cultural and language differences. My meeting with O'Jack made me realize that every encounter with everyone I interact with throughout every day of my life is really a spiritual experience. When I look at my life from that perspective, I am able to slow down and appreciate everyone I meet, the clerk at the grocery store, the teller at the bank, even the stranger whose eyes meet mine as we pass on the street. Now that I am retired and not in such a frenzy to constantly do, do, do, I am able to take the time to recognize these spiritual encounters. The possibilities are endless and the rewards are immeasurable.

—*Beth Davidson*

I find such joy in making a spiritual connection with the new people I meet.

"Perfect love sometimes does not come
until the first grandchild."

—*Welsh proverb*

At a recent visit to my physical therapist, a woman was having treatment for a tear in her shoulder and she was in a lot of pain. We began talking and she said sarcastically, "Yup, the joy of aging!" and I had to laugh as I was in the process of writing this book. I asked her what she did to find joy in aging and she answered her grandchildren. She has seven grandchildren and has a wonderful time with them, always looking forward to seeing them as well as they looking forward to seeing her.

If you don't have grandchildren yet, you can certainly look forward to them. And if you don't have any and might not have any, there are so many other ways you can find joy in aging. T. Berry Brazelton said, "A grandchild is a miracle but a renewed relationship with your own children is even a greater one."

If you don't have grandchildren, you can find great joy in friendships, volunteering, or learning something new. You could help at school, at children's camps, or babysit.

*There are so many ways
to find joy in aging today.
I pray I keep a
positive attitude.*

giving love

did you know?

"Positive social support is associated with better mental health, cardiovascular health, immunological functioning, and cognitive performance in older adults."

—*Louis Cozolino*

One person I know told me that she found joy in aging when she and a bunch of friends who were around the same age (she was 63) went on a camping trip once a month. They found a campground close to where they lived so they would not have to travel far, and everyone brought food so they would not have to cook. They laughed, played cards, and had a wonderful time. She told me her mother is in her 80s and has had friends die. She keeps making friends with younger people who keep her energized.

Another way to stayed connected socially is to plan to live in a 55-plus community, where there are many activities to choose from and people to be with, one or two pools, exercise equipment, and rooms for cards and other games and parties and banquets.

Clubs, travel groups, and volunteering keep us well connected as well.

Aging can be just a new way to begin.

"Some believe Spiritual Health is an art of healing:
the ultimate medicine, a remedy that cures your inner
sight as well as your spirit. There are those who
believe it also provides you with the capacity of loving
yourself unconditionally and reconnects you to
your talents and gifts, which helps in
feeling fulfilled with your life."

—*Karen Kleinwort*

*I am doing everything I can today to have
a healthy mind, body, and spirit*

"Love is the ultimate meaning of everything around us.
It is not a mere sentiment; it is truth; it is the
joy that is at the root of all creation."

—*Rabindranath Tagore*

L ove begins with ourselves. It is very simple. Anything that blocks us from feeling love lies within us and how we relate to ourselves. By the second half of our lives, most of us have built many barriers to love to protect us from being hurt. The accumulated experiences, the disappointments that didn't go the way we wanted, the unfulfilled dreams, the relationships gone sour, all lead to our shutting down unconsciously.

When we can't accept and love ourselves, exactly as we are, we can't accept and love anyone else.

It's time to let go. It's time to open up. It's time to be mindful of everything we tell ourselves that blocks us from accepting and loving ourselves. It's time to be free. It's time for my personal transformation.

*I am opening up today to let God remove
everything that is standing in the way of my completely
accepting myself just as I am, of my loving
myself, of my ability to love others.*

did you know?

In a published study, just eight weeks of mindfulness training was shown to create significant changes in regions of the brain associated with attention, memory, stress, and empathy. Two of these regions include the prefrontal cortex, which allows us to control and shift our attention, and the insula, which makes us more self-aware and empathic.

Mindfulness often fosters a sense of spirituality.

Some studies have shown that people who pursue some sort of spirituality live longer.

Neuroscientists have been able to pinpoint specific areas of the brain that are activated when people pray.

Nearly two out of every three U.S. medical schools now offer courses on spirituality.

Research has proven that meditation can positively modify brain activity, immune function, and the body's stress response, as well as lower heart rate and blood pressure, and can heal heart disease, diabetes, arthritis, and chronic pain.

Mindfulness is key to sharpening memory and staying mentally fit.

I am committed to meditate at least once a day
and to practice mindfulness as I go
through the rest of my day.

"A thought is harmless unless we believe it.
It is not our thoughts but our attachment to our
thoughts that causes our suffering."

—*Byron Katie*

Thoughts come in and go out of our minds. Where do they come from? We don't know. Where do they go? We don't know. Some come from our own perceptions and judgments and ideas from other people, and we believe that they are true.

Have you ever found that you disliked something as a child, only to find that changed when you became an adult? For example, maybe you looked at an oyster and thought you could never put it in your mouth. Many years later, you had the courage to try one and you liked it! If you held on to your early belief, you never would have discovered that you could like oysters.

Thoughts such as *How will I take care of myself when I am old? What if I don't have enough money? I hope I don't have to go into a nursing home.* We could live for another twenty or thirty years making ourselves miserable with these thoughts only to die quietly and peacefully in our sleep.

Mindfulness helps us to be aware of our thoughts and not get attached to them. Mindfulness helps us to see them and let them go. Mindfulness helps us to transform our lives from one of worry to one of peace and joy.

*Today I am going to be curious about my thoughts
as I watch them come into my mind and then disappear,
seeing that they have no substance in reality.*

"If nothing ever changed, there would be no butterflies."

—Author Unknown

For many years our once lovely orange tree has been failing, becoming sicker and sicker, until finally one half of the poor tree was bare of all leaves. I procrastinated having it cut down, hoping for a miracle that I knew wouldn't happen.

This tree was the home for my orchids which blossomed beautifully under its leaves. I had been told that orchids thrive hanging from the branches of trees as the shade protects them from the direct sun, and they would get enough water just by being outdoors. I didn't want to lose the orchids' wonderful home. I finally gave in, hired someone to remove the tree, and hung the orchids under the overhanging roof of my driveway.

In spite of all my resistance, in spite of my fear of change, the orchids are thriving. I planted a beautiful, healthy tree full of blossoms where my poor orange tree once grew.

So many times we fear change, only to find out that life flows just as it was meant to and most of our fears never happen.

The more we practice a combination of acceptance and letting go, the more joy we will find in our lives. As my friend Joann recently emailed me, "So, the world turns, sometimes with our help, mostly it just turns. I like the world and trust it today, just along for the big ride."

Today I trust that my life is flowing just as it was meant to flow.

"What a time to be alive!
There are no ideas that are totally tapped down,
no ideology is adequate to the tasks of this time.
So it is a time for really alive, innovative people.
I have my oar in the water with everyone else.
I am rowing in the direction I can....
It is great to be alive."

—*Fran Peavey*

*I am mindful of being really alive
as I live fully at every age.*

"Carpe diem!" (Seize the day!)

—Horace

Having had, for many years, the joy and the privilege of experiencing a way of life that focuses on the wise suggestion to "live in the day," I feel rather disconnected from the term "aging." For so many years of my life, I projected disasters into the non-existent future and consequently suffered much unnecessary, agonizing pain over imaginary situations and happenings. I also worried more about "getting old" when I was in my 30s, 40s, and 50s than I do now at almost the three-quarters of a century mark.

I certainly have not mastered the "living in the day" skill, but continue to work at it and experience much improvement as time goes on. I appreciate each day of life as a precious gift regardless of age. After all, we begin to "age" on the day of our birth. I am grateful as I realize how much I have learned in my life thus far, and also realize how little I really know. There is a sense of excitement in the knowledge that life has so much more to teach me and I am eager to learn. My hope is that I may "live gracefully" as long as I am in this world, one day at a time.

—Barbara Thomas

*Learning to live just one day
at a time, my life is rich and full
and open and free.*

my practice

"The real mindfulness practice is your life.
It's not about 45 minutes a day and the job is done.
It's about letting the practice spill over into every waking
moment of your life . . . you're no longer practicing
a technique. It becomes a way of being."

—*Jon Kabat-Zinn*

It is important to do the formal practice, which is sitting and quietly calming your mind for a regular period each day, preferably in the morning. You can concentrate on your breath or a phrase, whichever works best for you. By training your mind this way, it will become more and more natural to bring your awareness to the rest of your day. You will be calmer, more peaceful, happier, and healthier, just to name a few of the perks.

*Not only does it feel so good
to be a daily meditator, but it also
is helping me be healthier
and more spiritual.*

"You've reached the stage in your life
when you can be anything you want to be.
Well, except young!"

—*Carlton Cards*

*It feels wonderful to express all aspects of
myself and be completely me today!*

"A child's world is fresh, innocent, new,
full of wonder and excitement. It is unfortunate that
for many of us that vision for what is awe inspiring
is dimmed as we grow older. If I had influence
over the good fairy who blesses all children, I would
ask her gift to each child in the world be this:
a sense of wonder so indestructible that it would
last through all the years of their lives."

—Rachel Carson

*I pray that I can always have a sense of wonder,
that my heart will always be open to the
joys and miracles of our world.*

"Whether you're up or you're down,
whether you're confident or unsure, listen
to your heart. For your heart
knows why you're here."

—*Ralph Marston*

As we grow older there are going to be days, weeks, months, or even longer when we experience a variety of physical, mental, and spiritual states. Actually, this happened when we were younger as well, but the ones in our future may be more difficult to go through. There are more aches and pains, more limitations, more losses.

No matter what we are going through, there is a purpose for us on this planet. Mindfulness helps us to trust our inner guidance. Mindfulness helps us to follow our spiritual path.

*I connect with my Higher Power in my
morning prayer and meditation, and I know
that I am being led on my journey.*

"Habits of thinking need not be forever.
One of the most significant findings in psychology
in the last twenty years is that individuals
can choose the way they think."

—*Martin Seligman*

When talking to people about aging, many had positive things to say about it. Some looked forward to doing what they wanted to do after they retire, such as travel or write their memoirs. Others thought of it as a time to volunteer or to spend more time with family and friends. Yet there were some who dreaded aging. One person said that there is nothing good about aging!

It has been said that how we think about aging will be how it is for us. Recent tests have proven that a positive attitude about aging improves our immune system. This is very important. Consider how you feel about aging.

Martin Seligman, professor of psychology, has shown that optimism can be learned. And optimists do better than pessimists in almost every aspect of life, including how well their immune systems function.

It is impossible to keep two opposite thoughts in mind at the same time, and the impact of a negative thought can be cancelled by thinking a positive one.

It is exciting to know that how I think about aging will be how I experience aging. I choose to have a positive attitude and look forward to experiencing joy as I grow older.

"Healing begins not where our pain is taken away, but where it can be shared and seen as part of a larger pain."

—*Henri J. M. Nouwen*

There is a wonderful Buddhist practice called Tonglen. It is a method for connecting with suffering and transforming it, ours and that which is all around us, everywhere we go. The essence of the practice is to breathe in the suffering of another person and to breathe out openness, freshness, loving-kindness, compassion, and healing. For example, if we are angry, we can get in touch with our anger, breathe in what it feels like to be angry, breathe out patience and forgiveness to myself and to all the people in the world who are feeling angry and projecting it on to others. We can also do this for someone we know is sick or is suffering. We can breathe in their sickness or their suffering and breathe out healing energy to everyone who is sick or suffering in the world.

One day my partner and I were having an argument. I can't even remember what it was about. I remembered Tonglen and just stopped. I breathed in all my anger, really felt it, and breathed out healing to everyone in the world who might be angry at their partner in that moment. I couldn't help but smile, feeling connected with them all. I was completely released from my anger.

When I realize that everything I feel, others are feeling;
that all the good feelings I want for myself such as life and joy
and happiness, others want as well. This helps me to know
that we are all connected in what we feel and how we act,
and whatever happens to me as I grow older, I am not alone.

It's incredible how
much younger
and lighter
I
feel
when I
live
mindfully
throughout
the day

"When we live in the present, joy arises for no reason.
This is the happiness of consciousness that
is not dependent on particular conditions.
Children know this joy."

—*Jack Kornfield*

*It fills me with great joy to have given up
all regrets from the past and all fears of the future.
Right now, in this present moment,
it is perfect.*

"If we don't practice, we don't have enough
of the energy of mindfulness to take care of our
fear and anger and the fear and
anger of our loved ones."

—*Thich Nhat Hanh*

For so many of us, fear and anger have accumulated over the years and we have become masters at hiding it, even from ourselves. It sometimes surprises us and slips out. Someone can push our buttons. The stock market is down for a month. You see a picture of an ex-spouse or a boyfriend or girlfriend.

Mindfulness gives us the courage to look deeply at all our hidden feelings, bringing them to the surface and nurturing them to understand them, and heal them through faith and compassion.

*I am so grateful that the practice
of mindfulness can bring me so much
peace, healing, and joy.*

God grant me the serenity
To forget the people I never liked anyway,
The good fortune to run into the ones I do,
And the eyesight to tell the difference.

—Author unknown

> "Bad habits are like chains that are too light
> to feel until they are too heavy to carry."
>
> —*Warren Buffet*

Over the years we develop many ways to search for joy. If we don't like how we feel, we look for instant change. Feeling irritable, unhappy, down, or bored we go in many different directions until we find the quick fix. Some of us find solace in alcohol or drugs. Others might look to shopping or eating or sex or gambling to feel better. Any of these might work . . . for a while. Soon they become addictive. Without our being aware, we become hooked. And we want more until we are in trouble.

Why not take some time today to look deeply into the habits that you might have developed that pull you down. Pray for the willingness to be honest with yourself. Learn to stay with feelings that you usually try to escape. Be mindful and honest about what is going on. Stop and bring your awareness to your breath three times. Try journaling or talking about what is going on.

Perhaps you need help if you can't stop on your own. Talk to someone you trust about it. We're never too old to let go of bad habits that keep us from the joy of life.

Today I pray for the honesty and willingness
to not run away or avoid what is going on in my life.
I choose to be real in the moment and accept life on life's terms,
and God gives me the courage to do this when I ask.

"We can't always like everyone, but we can love them."

—*Author unknown*

I received an email from a friend recently letting me know that someone I had worked with, yet I hadn't seen in over twenty years, had died. I remember thinking that I was sorry she died so young. She was only 59. Yet my memories of her were not pleasant. We had not gotten along.

I was aware that I didn't want to remember our unpleasant times together, and it got me to thinking about how to deal with a situation like this. How could I let go of my memories and feel at least neutral when her name came up?

Forgiveness came to mind first, but I really knew there was nothing to forgive. Acceptance then came to mind. We really can't always like everyone. We are not saints. But we can accept our differences. She and I just had different ways of doing things. I prayed for the willingness to accept our differences and I began to feel much better. I realized I had judged her and felt self-righteous. Just being willing to let go made me feel better.

Are there people in your past that you didn't like? Are there people you still resent? If we are to grow older with a peaceful heart, we have to be willing to let go of feelings such as these that block us from love.

It feels good to know that with willingness and prayer, I can let go of my judgments and feel at peace with everyone.

"What lies behind us and what lies before us are tiny
matters compared to what lies within us."

—*Ralph Waldo Emerson*

E merson also wrote that life is a journey, not a destination.
As we age, some of us become more fearful as we think of
the destination, the end coming close—all of the things we fear
about aging are not far away. If we are on a spiritual journey,
developing faith and trust that our life has a purpose and that we
are a part of a much larger purpose, that we are connected to each
other in a very profound way, then we will live each day with joy.

We can stay right here, now, in this moment, and ask ourselves:

How do I want to spend the rest of my years?
What does my heart want?
What is really important?
What are the longings of my soul?

Maybe these questions aren't important to you. Maybe you
think you have already done enough with your life and now you
only want to play and rest. There is no right or wrong way.

Let your heart lead the way.

As I meditate I will look deeply into my heart
and pray to discover what I am to do with this day.
It takes the pressure off trying to figure it out for myself.

"Character cannot be developed in ease and quiet.
Only through experience of trial and suffering can the
soul be strengthened, ambition inspired,
and success achieved."

—*Helen Keller*

Over the years we all experience some form of suffering, whether it be through sickness or loss. Wise people have written about this through the centuries from the Bible, "Suffering produces endurance, and endurance produces character, and character produces hope" (Romans 5: 3–4), to the Buddha, "I teach one thing and one only: that is, suffering and the end of suffering," to Helen Keller. It is said that the place where a bone breaks and is healed is stronger than it was before.

While going through our times of suffering it doesn't help very much for someone to tell us that we will be stronger when the time has passed, but in truth, we are. There is a Jewish proverb that suggests, "I ask not for a lighter burden, but for broader shoulders."

Prayer and meditation can help us with our times of suffering. Talking about what we are going through with a trusted friend can be a great support.

Journaling is always a wonderful source of relief. It is important to remember that the more we resist, the greater we suffer. It helps to accept that, yes, there is suffering and to be very gentle with ourselves when going through it.

No matter what I am going through,
I know that with the help of prayer and meditation,
I will be led to a place of healing and peace.

"I don't want to get to the end of my life and
find that I have lived just the length of it, I want
to have lived the width of it as well."

—*Author unknown*

A h, the joy of aging mindfully or perhaps sometimes mind-
lessly! The journey for me has been one of joy throughout
my life . . . I was given the gift of "seeing the good" in everything,
everyone, and every circumstance.

"It's all good" is my mantra for *LIFE*. In reflection, I know in
my heart of hearts it was "mindfulness" that kept and keeps the
vision of goodness ever present within me.

I have become mindful of "being"; simply feeling the soft
breeze of the palm trees or the permeable scent of sweet jasmine,
or gazing at the sparkling crystals dancing on the Gulf waters.
The simplicity of Mother Nature caresses my being with happiness and brings me to the "present moment," filling me with
gratitude for being in my skin. Living life "my way" is truly a
reward for tending to my dreams both emotionally and spiritually throughout my life. Being all right with "me" and those all
around me has allowed me to experience grace beyond measure.
Through love and forgiveness, I have found the serenity that
beckons us all, and through mindful recognition.

—*Eileen Kemp*

I allow the gift of mindfulness to enter my soul.
I accept it in joy. I am at peace, and I am grateful!

*I can be more aware of my negative thoughts
and replace them with positive ones!*

OCTOBER

OCTOBER 1

time for reflections

It's incredible how
much younger
and lighter
I
feel
when I
make an
intention in the
morning to
live
spiritually
and
come from
a place
of love.

"If I can stop one heart from breaking,
I shall not live in vain; if I can ease one life
from aching, or cool one pain, or help one
fainting robin unto his nest again,
I shall not live in vain."

—*Emily Dickinson*

Is there something I can do for someone else today? It does not have to be a big something . . . just something that warms my heart?

Am I using the wisdom I have acquired to help others?

Am I being generous with my time and my abilities?

"That nothing is static or fixed, that all is fleeting and impermanent, is the first mark of existence. It is the ordinary state of affairs. Everything is in process. Everything—every tree, every blade of grass, all the animals, insects, human beings, buildings, the animate and the inanimate— is always changing, moment to moment."

—*Pema Chödrön*

Age 25: Sit on the floor and cross the legs. Keep the shoulders back. Palms open on the lap. Breathe in the nose and out the mouth. Visualize peacefulness. Age 50: Sit comfortably in a chair and uncross the legs. Keep the shoulders slightly rounded with palms down on the knees. Breathe in the mouth and out the nose. Visualize calmness. Age 60: Gravity has already relaxed most of the body so sit! Or recline if you prefer. Breathe easily. Try not to fall asleep.

After forty years of differing meditation techniques, endless teachers from distinct practices, and countless instructions that often contradicted one another, my aching joints and wandering mind finally found peace. In that flash point when the heart opens knowingly and the mind becomes still, I slid into a daily practice that now keeps me centered, focused, and in a state of gentle gratitude.

Age 65: This daily practice is a gift from spirit that came after all those years of experience. It's a gift of breath, of sound, and of timelessness. It starts each day and holds me attentive, no matter the circumstances unfolding around me.

In that daily meditation I am present and alive to the re-Union.

—*Jo Mooy*

I am so grateful my daily meditation practice brings me such peace and joy.

"Loving-kindness and compassion are the
basis for wise, powerful, sometimes gentle, and sometimes
fierce actions that can really make a difference—
in our own lives and those of others."

— *Sharon Salzberg*

Most of us to have times of struggle or suffering. Loving-kindness is a wonderful technique to use in these down times.

I had a knee replacement during writing this book. It took away most of my strength. I was very tired. I had a deadline and there were times when I was concerned as to whether I could finish on time. I began to practice loving-kindness for myself:

May I be happy.

May I be peaceful.

May I be gentle, loving, and compassionate with myself.

May I be understanding and accepting of exactly where I am now.

May I be free from suffering.

It lifted my mood and helped me stay positive and not let my pain pull me down into self-pity and depression. I stopped pushing myself. I did what I could do, without expecting more, and soon I got back into my natural flow.

Today I am sending loving-kindness to myself, those I love, those with whom I have difficulty, and then to everyone in the world, as I practice healing and compassion and peace.

good to know

Scientists spent approximately eight years following over 200 middle-aged and older volunteers with mild forms of high blood pressure, and they found that those who meditated regularly had a 23 percent lower mortality rate.

No matter how busy I am,
I am committed to meditate every day.

"Journaling . . . the cure for grief in motion."
—*Elbert Hubbard*

Journaling can help us express ourselves and free ourselves from our pain. Here are some suggestions to help you:

- Have a quiet room and privacy.
- Plan to have enough time, plenty of paper, and pens or pencils.
- Light a candle or use mood music.
- Write a focusing statement such as: "I know my higher power is with me as I write."
- Hang a DO NOT DISTURB sign on the door.
- Turn the phone ringer off.
- Use a notebook with a color that is appealing.
- Do not worry about grammar or punctuation. Let it flow.
- Keep your journal in a safe place.
- STOP when you're overwhelmed and close the book.
- Write the word BREATHE at the top of every page.

On the front page write:

STOP! THIS IS THE PERSONAL JOURNAL OF:
(your name here)
DO NOT READ ANY FURTHER
UNLESS YOU HAVE BEEN GIVEN
FULL PERMISSION

*With each page I feel freer and freer
to live a life of joy and peace.*

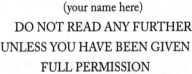

my journal

> "Agitation in the body and mind creates
> dis-ease and accelerates aging. Deep rest in body
> and mind reverses biological age."
>
> —*Deepak Chopra*

I read somewhere that a year of mediation slows down the aging process for a year. I don't remember where I read it and I do not even know if this is true, but I used to have some fun when I talked about mindfulness in schools. When I was teaching the kids in the third through the sixth grade, I would tell them that I had been meditating for many years and that since every year of meditation slows down the aging process for a year, I was really 106 years old. Gullible as they were at that age, some would look at each other with big eyes and say, "Wow! Is she really?"

While this statement that mindfulness slows the aging process one year might be an exaggeration, it is a well-known fact that stress affects many parts of our bodies, aging us more quickly, whereas mindfulness heals, reversing our biological age. It feels wonderful to know that a great deal of how I feel when I age has a lot to do with whether or not I meditate!

I am so grateful I have a technique that not only makes me feel good but also heals my mind and my body. I intend to make meditation a regular part of my day no matter what is going on in my life!

"One of the most important benefits of mindfulness is attentiveness to what is happening in your body, your mind and your environment—being present to what is happening with you, in you and around you at a particular moment in time . . . having less emotional reactivity and more stability of mind. Not overacting emotionally brings greater mental clarity, which is healthy in and of itself."

—*Susan Bauer-Wu, Ph.D.*

There are so many things we can do to practice mindfulness during the day. Here are just a few:

When the phone rings, wait for three rings before answering it. Breathe in and out, being aware of your breath as you wait.

When walking from the car to the house, practice walking slowly, mindful of your feet as they touch the ground.

STOP three or four times during the day and breathe in and out three times. Use the same technique when any negative or stressful feelings come up.

When driving, be aware of your hands on the steering wheel, your body as it sits in the seat, your foot as it touches the gas pedal.

When in a conversation with someone, be fully present. Listen carefully, without letting your mind go to any judgment or thought of how you will respond.

Take the time to sit with mindfulness meditation twenty minutes at the start of your day.

How wonderful it is to be able to bring peace and joy to any moment by simply being aware of my breath.

> "For everything there is a season, and a time
> to every purpose under heaven."
>
> —*The Bible, Ecclesiastes*

Studying nature can teach us so much about our own lives. Just as there is constant change in the universe, so are there predictable consistencies in nature's changes. We can depend on the changes of seasons, of spring following winter, of fall following summer. We can count on the tides going in and out twice in every 24 hours. The moon makes predictable cycles as does the Earth spinning around the Sun.

While these changes are taking place, beyond our control and without any help from us, nature is busy acting out in a seemingly inconsistent manner, affecting our lives through rainbows and hurricanes, earthquakes and sunshine, heavy rains and drought.

We have our own highs and lows, ups and downs, joys and sorrows. Taking time to be alone with nature, connecting with a power greater than ourselves on a regular basis, can be an anchor in times of difficulty, a comfort in times of pain, and a friend in times of joy and happiness. There is reassurance in knowing that the mountains and oceans are always there as a refuge, to pacify and sustain us.

Life happens. Change happens. We age. We grow older. We are part of a much bigger plan. William Wordsworth tells us to "come forth into the light of things, let Nature be your teacher."

Today I affirm that nothing is forever and I can find strength no matter what is going on in my life, in nature, and in God.

*I can focus on everything I am
grateful for in my life.*

Living mindfully in the present,
we can become aware of the characteristics we
have that block us from being fully alive.
As we become mindful of emotions such as anger,
jealously, craving, we can turn them into
thoughts that bring us joy such as love
and peace and compassion.

*I pray for the insight to transform
my thoughts that create suffering to
thoughts that create joy.*

No Mud
No Lotus

—Zen saying

We have all suffered, some more than others. There are those of us who have been abused in childhood. There are those of us who have lost loved ones. We carry deep images of pain with us. It's very rare to reach adulthood and not to have suffered at all, even if it is only in our mind's interpretation of what had happened to us.

The more we deny our suffering, push it down, and refuse to see it, the more our pain deepens and deepens and has no chance to heal. Instead, we need to have the courage to allow our suffering to come to the surface and acknowledge it. One form of healing is to give lots of love, compassion, and understanding to our inner child, the one who has suffered. We need to do this often and soon our suffering will become less and less painful.

healing my inner child

Today I am giving love and compassion and healing to my inner child. It feels so good to know I am in the process of healing.

> "Mindfulness is not about fixing anything,
> but about seeing things as they actually are and
> then being in a wise relationship, even
> if it is difficult or painful."
>
> —*Jon Kabat-Zinn*

It's important not to expect that the practice of mindfulness will give us a peaceful and problem-free life. It certainly will bring us peace, but life will still continue to happen. We will still have joys and sorrows, health and sickness, birth and death. What mindfulness offers is a way of being with whatever occurs but not getting caught up in the drama of it. Not creating stories about it. Not holding on to it but detaching from it.

We learn that we are okay, no matter what, and that we are being guided by a power greater than ourselves. Mindfulness connects us with this power so that we can handle whatever happens in our lives.

It is so freeing to know that I do not have to
be in charge of everything that happens in my life.
With the help of mindfulness I can deepen
my connection with the God of my
understanding and let go.

"The kiss of the sun for pardon,
The song of the birds for mirth,
One is nearer God's Heart in a garden
Than anywhere else on earth."
—*Dorothy Gurney*

Giving up the garden was one of the hardest things for me to consider when we thought about selling our house. How could I leave without seeing what came up the next spring? Would the tulips, the crocuses, and the daffodils bloom? Would there be more flowers from the same bulbs? Would the perennials be larger?

Thoughts such as these kept popping up until, gratefully, I accepted that I was gardening for the pleasure of gardening. Enjoying each moment. Feeling and smelling the earth, studying the best place to plant the next bulb, simply being out of doors, and aware of the miracle of growth, the continuity of life, and how we are all part of the same miracle.

I finally came to the "aha!" realization that when we moved, I could have a patio or a deck and plant flowers and vegetables in containers. This taught me so many lessons! I came to see that I didn't have to depend on the old way in anything I did, just because I always did it that way. I could, if necessary, downsize, find a new way, and enjoy nature just as much on a smaller scale.

Whether I water a small plant on my windowsill,
or spend hours weeding out of doors,
I will cherish my time with my garden today!

"Nature is the living, visible garment of God."

—*Goethe*

After writing at my computer for some time one beautiful May morning, I knew it was time to stop. I had a huge to-do list and time was running out. The thought of doing those things began to overwhelm me. I had visions of throwing all my papers across the room.

The outdoors was calling me. My garden and the new plants were calling me. The soft spring breeze said, "Come on out! Feel me on your face. Let me blow your cares away. Put your hands in the earth and get close to God." I gave in to the fact that I was accomplishing nothing by staying in.

As soon as the decision was made, I felt a tremendous sense of relief. I was going outside! I was going to use solitude as a mind-stopping, pressure-releasing natural tranquilizer. No lofty goals of spirituality or being at one with the universe. No looking within to connect with my inner strength. I was simply being alone in a place I loved, finding joy doing the things I loved to do. Escaping to the wonderful world of peace and quiet of the out of doors.

Nature is everywhere and always available. And it's easy to be mindful when we are in nature. We can just be aware of each moment as we enjoy its gift.

Today I am going to take time alone with nature
and do something I love just for me.

"You are the only person who thinks in your mind.
You are the only power authority in your world.
You get to have whatever you choose to think."

—*Louise Hay*

It is so good to know that what I choose to think, I feel.
Today I intend to think loving and positive thoughts because
this is what I choose to feel. As soon as I am mindful of
a negative or unpleasant thought, I am letting
it go and replacing it with loving
and positive thought.

> "In the beginner's mind there are many possibilities,
> but in the expert's there are few."
>
> —*Zen Master Shunryo Suzuki*

Maintaining "beginner's mind" is the work of mindfulness practice. As soon as we think we are an expert, as soon as we think we know it all, there is no room to be open and learn to see things as they really are.

Today I went for a walk. I don't need to go anywhere special to walk—my neighborhood and yours are filled with walkable spaces. Today, the wind blustered in from the south, the sky was filled with clouds and grayish light. Yesterday, slightly breezy, the sun beat down on the same path. Today, the upswept leaves tumbled to greet me as I traveled north. Yesterday the leaves rested. Today, many creaky sounds behind me might announce a bike about to pass or branches rubbing together. Yesterday my path was filled with friendly bikers and each bell announced the passing of a bike. As I walked today, in and out of present moment awareness, a raindrop hit my chin—a mindfulness bell announcing a change in my environment. Was it the first drop around me? This I know—that I don't know. That single, not solitary, raindrop returns me to beginner's mind—to this walk, to this raindrop, to this temperature, to this body—always different, always new.

—*Betsey Nelson*

*I experience great joy when I stay open to
the miracle of each moment. It feels so good to let go of
all my concerns I have about growing older.*

I have lived many years.
I have learned many things.
I pray I may take all my knowledge
and experience
to help wherever
and whomever
I can.

> "Your daily habits and routines . . .
> are either hurting or helping your brain."
> —*Daniel Amen*

Mindfulness can help us be more aware of the things we do that lead to an unhealthy brain. We can be more aware of the things we do which lead to stress and stop them. We can be aware of the wrong foods we eat, our lack of exercising, and our negative, pessimistic thoughts. We can be aware when we live in the past, holding on to "should haves" and resentments. We can be aware when we live in the future with fear, worry, and projection.

Daniel Amen tells us that a healthy brain is more thoughtful, playful, insightful, romantic, and productive. He says if we have healthy habits we are able to think well into our later years. These habits include healthy sleep, no cigarettes, and mild or no drinking. It includes giving up excessive television, video games, computer use, and cell phone time. He tells us what we eat on a regular basis helps or hurts out brain. It has also been proven that people who only work out at the gym and do not exercise their minds have less healthy brains than those who work both their bodies and their brains.

It is so wonderful to be living in an age where we know
so much about healthy aging. I am committed to do all I can to
help myself so that I will age in the best way possible.

> "The years teach much which
> the days never knew."
> —*Ralph Waldo Emerson*

I am mindful that the younger people around me do not perceive me the way I perceive myself. When I was young, I thought that older people did not have much to say, and if they did, it might be outdated and feeble at best. They would want me to listen to them reminisce about the old days and I would be bored. I can see this in the eyes of younger people today as they discount me or treat me as if I am invisible. As I age I realize that my thinking is as youthful as ever, tempered with a lot of experience and hopefully some wisdom. Although I speak less often now in public than in the past, I am up on the news and trends and would have something to say if invited to do so. In fact, I believe most young people would be surprised at how open and liberal senior thoughts can be. I accept that younger people are just as busy with their own agendas as I was with mine "back in the day." It has become enough to know the things I know and not feel the need to express myself to everyone.

—*Diana Smith*

*It gives me great joy and freedom
to know that it's not important
what others think of me!*

311

"Years may wrinkle the skin, but to give up
enthusiasm wrinkles the soul."

—*Samuel Ullman*

*It's a joy to know that I can have fun and do
new things as long I don't let my mind tell me I can't!
Today I am open to whatever comes my way,
and that is exciting.*

Short, Informal Walking Meditation

Slow, mindful walking is a wonderful way to practice being in the moment, releasing stress and just plain slowing down. There are so many times we can practice this. Just walking from one room to the other with awareness to every step can give us the same peace as when we breathe in and out mindfully three times.

You can practice a slow meditative walk as you are walking to and from your car. This can be a wonderful transition from work to home or vice versa, leaving work at work or concerns you have at home by being in the present moment. Rather than being off somewhere in your head, lost in your thoughts, thinking and planning, bring your full awareness to the present moment. Feel your feet in your shoes, touching the ground, and be with each step. Nothing else is important in this moment.

Even on a crowded street, walking meditation can help to slow you down, to become centered again, and keep you in the present moment. This can bring you a deep sense of peace. Wherever you are, there is often an opportunity to use mindful walking as an opportunity to slow down, clear your mind, and become centered.

It is so peaceful and centering to simply slow down and bring my awareness to each step that I take, each breath that I take, each object that awakens my senses.

mindful techniques

"To see a world in a grain of sand,
And a heaven in a wild flower,
Hold infinity in the palm of your hand,
And eternity in an hour."

—*William Blake*

One wonderful way to practice mindfulness is to take ten or twenty minutes each day and do nothing but be mindful of everything that is before you. If it is the right season, walk outside and examine a flower, a grain of sand, a blade of grass, clouds, a drop of water.

Pick up a stone or a shell and examine the details. Turn them over in your hand. Smell them. Feel their texture. Watch a butterfly or insect flit. In winter, you can watch a snowflake from your window or go outside and let them drop on your tongue.

You will be amazed how quickly the time flies, how peaceful you feel, and how your busy mind becomes quiet.

Today I am giving myself the gift of stopping and being completely in the present for at least ten or twenty minutes and feeling the joy of each moment.

"Inside every older person is a younger
person wondering what happened."

—Jennifer Yane

I am no longer young. How wrenching that is to say. The cankerous joints and leaky hoses won't let me forget.

But who doesn't want to live to old age? I did. My warmest memory of old age is of my Gramma Kertes in her rocker, crocheting, her canary belting out an unnamed but familiar aria on the sun porch. I was away at college when diabetes took her toes, then her sight. Her last years were spent in claustrophobic darkness. I never knew what happened to the canary.

Much like Gramma in her last years, I seem to have gone through life wearing dark glasses and tapping a white cane in front of me. At times I thought I knew where I was going and at times I was totally lost. It's largely a mystery to me as to how I got to this place: old.

So what now?

My guess is that my dotage will be about as predictable as my earlier life has been. Unlike my youth with its great expectations, the trick now is to just let it unfold.

—Jim O'Donnell

*Aging is very simple when I simply endure
the rough, savor the sweet, and let go.*

did you know?

Mindfulness often fosters spirituality, and
several studies have found that people who pursue
some form of spirituality live longer.

There are many definitions of spirituality but the one that speaks the strongest to me is "our relationship with ourselves, each other, and God."

To be spiritual does not mean that one has to be religious, although religion is spiritual. Spirituality is really an inner path enabling a person to discover the essence of their being and to choose the values by which they want to live.

Spirituality includes meditation, prayer, and contemplation. Neuroscientists have been able to pinpoint specific areas of the brain that become activated when people pray. The meditative state of intense prayer has been found to lower blood pressure and heart rate, which reduces the body's stress response. In one study at Duke University, with over 800 medical in-patients, they found that patients who prayed had higher cognitive function. Nearly two out of three U.S. medical schools now teach a course on spirituality, which certainly tells us there is proof that spirituality helps us stay healthy.

I am deepening my spirituality each day
with prayer and meditation.

"Every day, think as you wake up:
Today I am fortunate to have woken up.
I am alive. I have a precious human life.
I am not going to waste it. I am going to use all
my energies to develop myself to expand
my heart out to others for the
benefit of all beings."

—*His Holiness the 14th Dalai Lama*

I am so grateful for the gift of this day.
I pray that I can do something good
for someone else today.

mindful techniques

> "The meditation process is to continually greet our experience, whatever it is, with mindful awareness, loving-kindness, and compassion."
> —*Sharon Salzberg*

As we continue to grow in age we can continue to be more mindful in many ways. With more years of life experience we can practice being mindful throughout our daily lives as well as during times of meditation. Knowing how the mind is likely to wander, we can focus on what we experience in each moment through our five senses—what we see, hear, touch, smell, taste. In addition, we can take the time to fully taste what we eat: see, smell, or taste even a single raisin.

One of Thich Nhat Hahn's books mentioned paying attention to what is around us. The suggestion was that even while driving and needing to be paying attention to driving safely, we might notice something we had not noticed in the past. I noticed that hydrants in different cities and towns were different colors, and I could tell which town or city it is, and even where the town line is, according to different colored hydrants.

—*Steffi L. Shapiro*

The time for mindfulness is any time. Today I am training my mind to be present to everything in my life, and I find such peace when I remember to do it.

mindful
techniques

"Between stimulus and response there is a space.
In that space is our power to choose our response.
In our response lies our growth and our freedom."

—*Victor Frankl*

One way to practice being in the moment with mindfulness is to bring your full awareness to your breath and notice the pause between your breathing in and your breathing out.

Breathe naturally and notice your in breath.

Be aware of the pause before you breathe in.

Notice as your breath exhales naturally.

Be aware of your breath as you breathe out.

Notice the pause between your out breath and your in breath.

Notice your breath as you breathe in.

Be aware of the pause before you breathe out.

Notice when your breath exhales naturally.

Repeat this a few times, being aware of the pause between each breath and how this pause gets longer.

This is a wonderful exercise to help you stay in the moment and become calm.

"I think the whole thing that keeps life whole is not
the actions of the great, but the little things, even to smile
or be kind at a particular moment. Do not think lightly of
these little gestures—it is their multiplication from
all over the world that creates heaven on earth."

—*Howard Thurman*

When I was in college I remember staying up for hours talking with friends about how we were going to make the
world a better place. We were young and enthusiastic and had
great energy and ideas. I can look back over the years and see that
I did accomplish some things that did help some people, although
they were not the huge changes we spoke about in college.

As we age, our energy slows down. We observe and learn more.
We see that massive changes in the world can sometimes take
decades and require the dedication of many people. Some of us
get discouraged and are inclined to do less. We let the younger
ones take our places.

This doesn't mean that each day we cannot make a difference
in someone's life, no matter how old we are. We can take a friend
to the doctor or store. Smile at someone in the supermarket. We
can send a card or an email to cheer someone up. There is always
something we can do to make someone else's life a little brighter.
We just need to keep our eyes and our hearts open.

*Today I am staying open to any chance I have to do something
for someone else. This gives me great joy.*

good news

"I begin each day with the intention to be of service.
Only by allowing our grief, outrage, longing,
pain and tears can we discover the wise heart
that can contain them all."

—*An African elder*

So many times we push away or deny our feelings, thinking we can't handle them or simply wanting to avoid their pain. One person I spoke with told me she put her unpleasant memories in a little box in the back of her mind so she won't feel them. As we grow older the unconscious harm of our denial causes us a multitude of diseases.

When we shut out or deny some feeling, we close our heart to feel other ones. No longer can we feel love and compassion at any depth. We lose precious experiences that life has to offer when we shut down the smallest part of ourselves.

By allowing ourselves to feel all our feelings we can remain healthy! We are stronger than we know. Freedom lies in acceptance, not denial.

There is such freedom and joy in knowing that
I have the capacity to feel all my feelings.

good news

It has been found that mindfulness meditation,
the mind-body therapy that refers to a state of awareness,
consciousness, and immediacy, not only de-clutters
the mind and helps attain inner peace but also reduces the
severity of menopausal hot flashes, claims a new study.
The findings of the study are published
in the journal *Menopause*.

This is very exciting news for women going through menopause and having a difficult time. The researchers found that
mindfulness training that included meditation and stretching
exercises not only enhanced sleep quality but also helped ease
stress and anxiety in women during menopause. Researchers
conducted an eight-week trial that helped ease stress and anxiety.
Women slept better and exhibited increased levels of well-being.
They were less troubled by their hot flashes, and improvement
persisted for over three months after they had completed the
classes. The women rated their hot-flash disturbances between
slight to moderate. Mindfulness meditation didn't reduce them
completely, just the severity of them.

*It is wonderful to know how many ways mindfulness
helps us with our minds, bodies, and spirits!*

NOVEMBER

It's incredible how
much younger
and lighter
I
feel
when I
take care
of
myself
mentally,
physically,
and
spiritually.

"Memory is a way of holding onto the things
you love, the things you are, the things
you never want to lose."

—*From the television show* The Wonder Years

My son, Bob, once gave me a wonderful pair of pantaloons. They were in style at the time, brightly striped and full cut, and popular with the young adults. I felt so pleased that my son thought me cool enough to wear them and I have a great picture of us standing together while I was wearing them.

A few years later I gave the pants away with a pile of other clothes. Sadly, a few years later, my son died. I had deep regret that I had given those pants away, as they were a wonderful reminder of the relationship I had with my son. I carried this regret for years and one day spoke to my meditation teacher about it. Wisely, he told me that the pants were just pants. What was important was the memory I had of the special relationship I had with my son. His words were so freeing because I will always have my memory.

So often we hold on to things. We clutter our closets and drawers and lives for fear of letting go. We hold on to regrets the same way. This isn't to say that memories aren't important. They are. They make up many happy times of our lives. It's the clinging we want to release and the fear that comes with it. What's important will stay in our hearts.

*I am becoming willing to let everything go that is not important
in my life today, including my fear of letting go. I am looking
forward to the freedom that comes with moving on.*

I smile at the person I see in the mirror.
I see changes that weren't there
last week or last year.
I smile
and I let
love fill my heart
for who
I am in this
moment.

"Doubt your doubts."

—A wise soul

A s we grow older and become aware that we have less energy, we may pull back on some of the things we enjoy doing. Things might take us longer to accomplish. We might be aware that our memory isn't what it once was. All this might lead us to feel less secure, to lose confidence in ourselves, and have lower self-esteem.

It's important that we see ourselves realistically and not expect we can do more than we can. It's just as important to see ourselves confidently, knowing that what we can do and how we do it is perfect for who we are right now. And it's just as important not to let ourselves fall into self-pity, feeling sorry for what we don't have and can't do. Let's not limit ourselves by having doubts.

I am exactly where I need to be in this moment and it is perfect!

*In the evening I can look back on my day and
see if I have to make amends to anyone.*

"The excitement of learning separates
youth from old age. As long as you're
learning, you're not old."

—*Rosalyn S. Yalow*

A very sweet, active, sharp woman in her 90s attended many of the same retreats that I have attended. At one retreat the leader suggested that we all look inside more deeply to gain greater insight to who we really are. She became very upset. She said she had meditated for many years and it had given her such joy. She was happy and in her happiness helped many other people. Now the leader wanted her to ruin, so she thought, the simple happiness that meditation had brought to her life. She suffered greatly that day, thinking that she was about to lose something very important to her. She was actually angry.

A few days later this same woman was radiant!

"How wonderful" she said, "that at my age I can look deeper and still learn more!"

No matter what age we are we can continue to grow!

"Chronic crowding, clutter, and
disorganization can lead to high levels of
the stress hormone cortisol which can impair
memory and concentration and aggravate a
wide range of age-related diseases."

—*Gary Small, M.D.*

*I am making time to simplify my life
and to discover who I am. It feels so good to know
that I am working toward becoming clutter-free.
Just thinking about this brings
me great peace and joy.*

"Usually we are much more interested in who
started the fire than in putting it out; we go on
and on about the object of our anger."

—Larry Rosenberg

Anger is one of the greatest hindrances to joy. When we were younger, our tempers were often short-fused and we had a tendency to just blurt out what we were thinking. As we age, many of us often keep our anger in, wanting to be seen as a serene person or wanting to be liked or not wanting to upset anyone.

So our anger stays inside.

He did this or she did that! The politician promised this! My son said he wouldn't drink! These are some of the messages playing over and over in our minds.

There's a different way to deal with our anger. Talk about it. Journal about it. Pray to have it removed. Ask yourself if you have any part in it. Ask if there is anything you can do about it. Ask yourself if this is how you want to feel.

You might have to speak directly to the person whom you feel is the source of your anger. The most important thing is that you are willing to let it go.

*Today I am willing to turn over anything and everything
that I am angry at to God and ask for it to be removed.
It feels so free to be willing to let go and let God!*

I am not
who I used to be,
nor can I do all
that I used to do.
I accept this today
and honor who I am
with love
and
respect.

"We may spend our lives seeking something
that is right inside us, and could be found if we
only stop and deepen our attention."

—*Tara Brach*

right here ♡

*Every once in a while I am spending
time to stop, breathe, bring my full awareness
to where I am in the present moment,
and feel the peace and the joy.*

"Today is life—the only life you are sure of.
Make the most of today. Get interested in something.
Shake yourself awake. Develop a hobby.
Let the winds of enthusiasm sweep through you.
Live today with gusto."

—*Dale Carnegie*

Author Karen Kleinwort suggests that one way we can improve our spiritual health is to learn a new hobby. We have been told by scientists that learning something new keeps our brain young. A new hobby is fun and can bring us joy. It is an opportunity to expand our skills by working through the challenges, and it feeds our spirit.

We can also take classes to learn new hobbies that put us in contact with other people. If not classes, we can work on our hobbies with others. It has been proven that people who socialize are happier, healthier, and live longer.

It's important to keep in mind that the point of a hobby is fun and relaxation. We don't have to be the best, do it perfectly, or get it done fast. Just take your time and enjoy the process!

I am looking forward to stretching my
mind and creativity as I find a
hobby that I can enjoy.

> "How we decide to behave as elders
> will in all likelihood become the most important
> challenge we will face in our lives."
>
> —*Ken Dychtwald*

When we are in the first half of our lives, most of us are busy with education, raising a family, working, and pursuing other interests. While some of this still continues into the second half, for some of us things slow down and we have more time.

We might begin to think about aging. We might come to the realization that we are not going to live forever. We might begin to think about how we want to live the second half of our lives.

When the time comes when we are a bit freer, for some it becomes a time of reflection, a time to nurture a deeper relationship with a power greater than ourselves, whether that be God or Spirit or the Buddha or Allah or something else. It is a time to deepen our spiritual practice, look at our values, and reflect on our life purpose. It is a time to examine what we have learned and what we have to contribute to the younger generations.

Aging is not just about what we will lose but what we have gained. It is a time for mindful spiritual reflection and reevaluation and finding a new way to find joy in our lives.

I'm taking time to meditate and pray on how to make
the best use of my life for myself and others.

Breathing in I'm aware of my breathing.
Breathing out I'm aware of my breathing.
Breathing in I'm aware of my breath going in my body.
Breathing out I'm aware of my breath leaving my body.
Breathing in I'm aware of my body just as it is . . .

all of it, with all the changes that have come
as I have been growing older.
In spite of some of the aches and pains
I'm filled with compassion for all my body can do.

I'm filled with gratitude.

I'm filled with joy.

The Infinite Joy of Not Knowing

Receiving a call from a doctor telling me I had cancer, I immediately felt pure fear running like ice water through my veins. Mindful that my brain was going off into fear and speculation, I breathed and calmed myself.

Thich Nhat Hanh is my teacher. He always advises us to ask "Are you sure?" If we answer "Yes," we need to check again. In the midst of one of the worst moments of my life, I found myself asking that question. The answer was, "No, I am not sure. This could be almost nothing or it could mean death." I didn't know. I immediately felt a deep peace. All that I knew for sure was that I had that moment. I knew that every moment was precious and I did not intend to waste any of my remaining moments in fear and speculation.

That was three years ago, and I have discovered that the awareness that I don't know what even the next moment, let alone the next month or year, holds for me, leaves my life open to infinite possibilities for joy.

—*Joanne Friday*

I am so grateful for the question "Are you sure?" It keeps me from projecting the worst and lets me stay in that nonthreatening, safe space of Not Knowing.

good to know

It's important to know that studies show elders
with positive ideas about aging have better memories and
health and, on the average, live 7.5 years longer than those
who have accepted negative stereotypes about aging.

I received a large variety of answers from a
questionnaire I sent out on aging. They went from
"There's nothing good about aging!" and long lists
of what goes wrong mentally and physically, to
inspiring positive ways of looking at aging.

Here's a wonderful list from my sister-in-law Sigrun Haase,
who has a great sense of humor. After having listed all the
things that have gone wrong with people she knows and with
herself, she writes:

How to cope? Well, there are some ways: To be able to say pretty
much what comes to mind. (After all, we are old and no one takes
us seriously.) Forget about us and think of others. Spoiling grand-
kids!!!!!!! No birthday celebrations: Denial, Denial, Denial! Travel—
if you can. Volunteering. Therapy to treat depression. Hobbies.
Forget looking into any mirror. Not having to compete. And above
all: humor and sharing with friends. It helps if one can look back on
life and say that one has been blessed.

*Today I am looking seriously at how I consider
growing older. I am making a list of all the positive ways
I can look at it and doing my best to let go of any
negative thoughts that pull me down.*

"Positive or 'feel good' emotions like appreciation,
compassion and joy are internal energy boosters.
They create hormonal mixtures that nourish
our cells and mind. They have also been shown to
prevent fatigue and slow down aging.
They regenerate and sustain us mentally,
emotionally and physically."

—*Kim Allen, Heartmath*

It brings me great joy to know that by being
mindful when I feel stressed, depressed, or upset,
I can turn the feeling around by thinking about something
for which I am grateful or someone for
whom I have compassion.

339

> "Without envisioning a new purpose for old age,
> we are creating an 'elder wasteland.'"
>
> —*Ken Dychtwald, Ph.D.*

Studies found that in 1998, 40 million retirees spent an average of 43 hours a week watching television. Ken Dychtwald paints a dismal picture if this doesn't change. As more and more Baby Boomers reach retirement, "an elder-wasteland will emerge in which more than 70 million couch-potato retirees drift through their mature years watching TV, surfing the 'net, wandering through malls, and playing various games while siphoning off society's resources."

While it's one thing to be happy that new findings in nutrition and medicine allow us to live much longer, we need to come to a different way of thinking about growing older.

Whatever age we are right now, if we do not have a healthy vision of what we would like to be and do when we retire, it's never too early to begin to think about it. And if we already are retired, it's time to examine the life we are living. Here are some questions you can consider: How can I play a meaningful role in society? How can I combine having a purpose or being of service with time for leisure? How can I make my life experiences as examples to help others?

*I am very mindful of how I can make my life a spiritual
and purposeful experience for as long as I am able.*

O ur meditation experience is not always the same. There will be days when you feel nothing but peace while other times your mind won't stop running everywhere. Most times it might be a mixture of the two with more emphasis on one or the other.

Sometimes you might even fall asleep. You'll doze. Your head might fall onto your chest. You might even dream.

It's all okay.

Just let it be as it is.

Next time will be different.

This time it is what it is.

And it is perfect.

good to know

"Fear knocked at the door. Faith answered.
And lo, no one was there."

—*Author unknown*

One of the biggest stressors we have when we think about the future is finances. Will I have enough money to pay my bills? Will I lose my house? Will I be able to have any fun? Will I be able to go into a decent retirement home? Will I have to live with one of my children?

With people living longer, the truth is many of us will outlive our savings. And there are some of us who haven't even been able to accumulate any savings. So many face economic uncertainty.

Trite as it may sound, all we can do is the best we can. We could come to a sudden, untimely death at any time, or we could live to one hundred years old. It is important not to project, but to let go of our fear, not to suffer by living in our head the future that isn't here. What we can do is practice living in the moment, deepen our spirituality, develop new and maintain old social connections, and trust we will know what to do when the time comes.

*It feels so good to turn my entire life over
to the care of God, and to live in
acceptance and peace.*

"Living humanly will be its own reward.
The person who has discovered the pleasures of truly
human living, the person whose life is rich in friendships
and caring people, the person who enjoys daily the
pleasures of good food and sunshine, will not need to wear
herself out in pursuit of some other kind of success."

—Harold Kushner

Most of us don't know the real joys of living until we are much older. Most of us pursue the perfect relationship, the perfect home, the perfect children, the perfect job, and so on. And gradually we come to discover that there never is a "perfect" one of these. The relationship will have fights, the home will have leaks, and the job will have problems.

But if we are lucky, gradually along the road of life, we will have discovered and been open to the warm and joyful feelings we have as our heart opens when we are grateful, when we are generous, when we help a friend along the way, when we pray and meditate and move closer to God and grow spiritually. Only when we experience these long-lasting joys do we know the true meaning and purpose of life.

*My heart is filled with joy and I am so grateful
to know that God is continuing to guide my
heart to the true purpose for my life.*

did you know?

In a recent study, scientists found that the people without heart disease were 60 percent more likely to see humor in everyday life. Other studies found that laughter improves our ability to tolerate pain. A regular dose of laughter such as reading the funnies or watching a sitcom may lift your spirits and boost your longevity. Other studies link watching a daily sitcom with lower blood pressure and improved heart beat regularity, both of which lower risks for heart attacks.

I'm letting everything go that makes me feel heavy,
dull, and burdened, and am making sure I see
or read one funny thing every day.

Today I am focusing on all the goodness in life,
all the blessings I have been given and the richness
of all the friends I have, and I feel great joy.

"Everything you think, you feel; and all that you feel
manifests to create the conditions of your life."

—*Ramtha*

I found this quote in a book I read over 25 years ago on a slightly yellow piece of paper where I had written: "This is the same path as the theory behind affirmations. Too Exciting!!!"

I had been using and teaching affirmations at this time, and this reinforced them. Affirmations have been proven to work. As we slow down and become more aware of our thoughts, we experience the connection between our thoughts and our feelings. We learn that we feel what we think. We can experience our ability to change how we feel by simply changing our thinking.

This does not mean that we should not feel our feelings. But when we find ourselves dwelling on painful or angry feelings of the past, we don't have to stay in that mood. We can change it.

If we are projecting growing older as a difficult time, we will suffer, and we might even create circumstances that make our fear true because we are limiting our thinking.

If we see growing older as a time for continued growth, for fun, a time to use our knowledge in some way for the good of others, then that is what we will create.

The choice is ours.

It is exciting to know that what I think, I feel,
and I can create thoughts that bring me joy.

> "Age should not have its face lifted,
> but it should rather teach the world to admire
> wrinkles as the etchings of experience
> and the firm line of character."
>
> —*Clarence Day*

A ging . . . what a gamut of emotions associated with that word. We usually think only of the aging that takes place in our bodies when we think of aging, because we go from baby soft to wrinkly old. But aging happens in our bodies, minds, and spirits.

My Mind . . . so much smarter, clearer, and so much more content.

My Spirit . . . so much more reliant on a power greater than myself, a calming, a peace, and a confidence never achieved by the younger me.

So all in all . . . I'll take the wrinkles, always making sure to nurture my skin as I do my mind and spirit.

—*Trisha Fritz*

*I pray I may continue to take care
of my mind, body, and spirit.*

my practice

"Sought through prayer and meditation to
improve our conscious contact with God, as we
understood Him, praying only for knowledge for
His will for us and the power to carry that out."

—*The 11th Step, Alcoholics Anonymous*

There are many special reasons for meditating in the morning,
the first being that we are connecting with the God of our
understanding when we wake up, and this makes it easier to stay
connected throughout the day.

Imagine that you are in a cold room with a heater in the center.
If you choose to turn it on in the morning you will be warm all
day. If you choose to wait until noon, you will be cold all morning.

In mindfulness we bring our full awareness to our breath.
Therefore, by beginning with this practice in the morning we are
more likely to remember to bring our awareness to both places
at other times during the day. At first we might remember only
when we are tense or suffering. We remember that breathing in
and out three times can bring us to a place of balance and serenity.
Soon we can remember to be mindful in our shower, and so forth.
Eventually, more moments of our days will be filled with mindfulness and we will feel serene more often.

*It feels so good to practice my mindful meditation first thing in
the morning, thus remembering that God is always with me and
my breath is always with me. There is great joy in knowing I just
have to stop, breathe in and breathe out, and feel the peace.*

"If your compassion does not include
yourself, it is incomplete."

—*Author Unknown*

There was a wonderful experiment conducted with three- and four-year-olds to teach them the meaning of kindness. Together with their teacher they collected food and brought it to different shelters where the homeless lived.

They quickly learned how good it made them feel when they practiced kindness. One little girl gave her flower to a stranger and then just started crying. The teacher asked her what was wrong and she said, "My heart just feels so good right now."

Just a flower to a stranger, just a smile to someone sad, just a hand when someone falls down. No big deal. No awards or praises. We feel the gift of the results of our actions right in our own hearts.

But are we leaving ourselves out? Can we be just as kind to ourselves? Why not take a deep look at how you treat yourself today and see what you can do for you.

Today I am taking time for me.
No matter how busy I think I am
I am stopping to do something
kind for myself because
I know I deserve it.

peace

"Walking meditation is meditation while walking . . .
When we practice this way, we feel deeply at ease, and our
steps are those of the most secure person on Earth.
All our sorrows and anxieties drop away, and peace and
joy fill our hearts. Anyone can do it. It takes only a little
time, a little mindfulness, and the wish to be happy."

—*Thich Nhat Hanh*

The wonderful part of walking meditation is that we are walking to experience each step, each breath, each moment. We walk slowly and in relaxed fashion. We put aside a special time with nothing to do but walk.

We feel our feet on the ground, our legs moving. We are not in the past or the present, only in this one moment this one step.

To help focus, we can count our steps to five and then begin again. We can say with one step "I have arrived," and with the next step "I am home." We can say with each two steps as they make contact with the ground, "Solid," "Stable."

We can concentrate on just four aspects of our step: lifting, moving, placing, and then shifting our weight to the other foot.

We concentrate on each step, therefore leaving the business of our thoughts, releasing our stress, and becoming more peaceful.

I am taking at least five minutes today to
practice mindful walking. It is amazing how
much peace and joy it brings me.

Over the years we build many habitual ways of responding and reacting that can cause great stress to our bodies. Whatever our age is now, we can find other methods for releasing this stress so as we age further we will retain our memory or at least not lose as much of it as we would if we didn't try to change.

Kim Allen from the Heartmath Institute tells us that when we have stress because of negative feelings, such as when we feel angry, anxious, worried, or frustrated, these negative emotions change the hormonal mix. She tells us that chronic stress bathes the body in stress hormones, which can speed up the biological aging clock, drain emotional resilience, and reduce physical vitality.

Positive or "feel good" emotions like appreciation, compassion, and joy are internal energy boosters. They create hormonal mixtures that nourish our cells and mind. They have also been shown to prevent fatigue and slow down aging. They regenerate and sustain us mentally, emotionally, and physically.

Mindfulness helps us to release stress so that we can be aware when we are having negative emotions and we can quickly change our thoughts to positive thoughts, such as appreciation, kindness, compassion, and love.

There is great joy in knowing that the more I practice mindfulness the more I am in charge of my thoughts. I am helping to keep my memory healthy as I age.

"When one door closes another door opens;
but we so often look so long and so regretfully
upon the closed door, that we do not see
the ones which open for us."

—*Alexander Graham Bell*

I t can be very painful to have to downsize as we grow older. It can be very painful to need to retire or lose our job. It can be very painful when friends move away or we move away from friends. So much of aging can be painful. But there is another side of all of this and we just need to be open to it. There can be an adventure in new places to live, a new job, volunteering opportunities, new friends, and other new opportunities. All we have to do is to stay open and trust that God is doing for us what we cannot do for ourselves.

*Today I feel at peace knowing that my future is
unfolding easily and effortlessly as long as
I stay open and not stuck in regrets.*

"Because thoughts come from the inside,
not the outside, what we think
determines what we see."

—*Jane Nelson*

C hanging thoughts from *What is wrong with me?* to *What is right with me?* can turn our mood around from unhappiness to joy. Mindfulness gives us the ability to be aware of our thoughts and change them before they change us.

im love

*Today I am practicing focusing on at least
one good quality I have that
makes me smile.*

> "A man can fail many times but he isn't a failure
> until he begins to blame someone else."
>
> —*John Burroughs*

Some of us still live in the past. We have "If only" and "I should have" thoughts. *If only my father hadn't been an alcoholic. If only women were promoted as quickly as men. If only that cop hadn't been there when I picked up speed. If only I was just a few inches taller I could have made it in professional basketball.*

Thoughts like these hold us back from moving forward. It has been shown that living in the past by blaming the past for our lack of success leads to great emotional stress. And stress damages us emotionally, spiritually, and physically.

Eric Fromm, M.D., wrote, "Man must accept responsibility for himself and the fact that only by using his own power, can he give meaning to his life."

Mindfulness helps us to be aware of our thoughts as we are having them. Being mindful allows us to see when we are living in the past or avoiding taking responsibility for our lives. Mindfulness helps up to stop and realize the damage we are doing to ourselves with our thoughts. We can then see the truth about a situation, change the way we react out of old habits, and move forward in a healthy way.

I am so grateful for the gift of mindfulness. It brings clarity and honesty to my life and this brings me great joy.

DECEMBER

It's incredible how
much younger
and lighter
I
feel
when I
am
other-centered,
helping
wherever
I
am
needed.

"If I'd known I was going to live so long,
I'd have taken better care of myself."

—*Leon Eldred*

*While there is no guarantee that I will be
happy and healthy as I age, there is a great deal
I can do to make the odds better on my side.
Today I am doing everything I can
to make this happen!*

good news

Neuroscientist Richard Davidson discovered that
when we're in a down mood our brain has high activity
in the right prefrontal area, just behind the forehead.
But when we're in an upbeat mood there's lots of
activity on the left side of the prefrontal area.

The good news: we can nudge our set point more to the left.

Richard Davidson and Jon Kabat-Zinn teamed up to study folks working at a high-stress biotech startup. Jon taught mindfulness to a group of the biotech workers and had them practice about half an hour a day for eight weeks. He measured their brains before and after. The result: at first their emotional set point was tilted toward the right—they were, after all, on a hectic, 24/7 schedule. But after eight weeks, the mindfulness group on average showed a greater tilt toward the left.

What's more, they spontaneously said that now they were in touch again with what they loved about their jobs with why they had gotten into the field in the first place.

In his blog, Jon Kabat-Zinn said that the change for a happier brain begins quickly, but to get the benefits, you've got to practice daily.

*I am so grateful I can practice mindfulness
daily and feel better, become happier and healthier,
live longer, and so much more!*

It's incredible how
much younger
and lighter
I
feel
when I
accept
and love
myself
just as
I
am
and stop
wishing
I were
like
someone
else.

did you know?

Many variables have contributed to aging gracefully.
In looking for one main factor, researchers found
that one of the greatest predictors of aging successfully
was the presence or absence of a sedentary lifestyle.

There are people who live until their 80s and 90s who are active and energetic, while others appear to be beaten down, and others don't make it to their 70s. Researchers have found that those who exercise have improved cardiovascular fitness, which reduced the risk of heart attacks and strokes. Exercise also raised cognitive performance and improved attention and problem solving.

What has this got to do with aging and mindfulness, you might be wondering? If we are mindful of how we are living, the thoughts we have, what we eat, and how we live our lives, we will want to do everything we can to be healthy. We will be mindful of what makes us feel good, what deepens our spirituality, what helps our brains and bodies function at their maximum level. We will be aware of the thoughts that create suffering and stress and be careful to let them go.

It is wonderful to know that science has finally caught up
with what wise people have known through the ages,
that all the things I do which help me feel better actually
help me to be healthier and happier as I age.

my practice

"Before the thought, you weren't suffering;
with the thought, you're suffering; when you recognize
the thought isn't true, again there is no suffering."

—*Byron Katie*

When we speak about our thoughts not being true, we really mean our concepts, our stories, our ideas about things. It doesn't mean a thought such as *It's raining out* isn't true. If it's raining, it's raining. A thought such as *It's hot* when it is 60 degrees might be true for someone who is used to living in a place where the temperature is 30 degrees. That wouldn't be true for someone who has just come from a place where the average temperature is 90 degrees. Everything is relative. Just because it is hot for me does not make it hot for you.

You might have the thought, *If only I had a better job with more money I would be happy when I retire,* or *It will be terrible to live alone as I get older,* or *There's a good chance I'll lose my memory when I get old because my father lost his.* You might think these thoughts are true and suffer over them.

Be mindful of your thoughts today. Question them. Ask yourself, "Is this true?" Is it true for just me or does everyone share this point of view? How would you feel if you let the thought go?

*Today I am letting go of all my stories that I build
around my fears. I'm resting comfortably in
what is true and feeling peace and joy.*

"My religion is very simple.
My religion is kindness."

—*His Holiness the 14th Dalai Lama*

I can honestly say I enjoyed each part of the many years of my life. There were so many small things that made me a person who always cared for others, especially those who were very different from me. As the years went on, and as I was growing older, life threw me many emotional curves: losing loved ones, sicknesses, and most of all loneliness. So rather than looking back, when life was easier and less lonely, what I can do now is try to live in the moment; the past is gone, the future is truly a mystery.

I look forward to the journey of my older years trying to make the people around me happy.

—*Claire Gelo*

*It feels so much better to plan what I can do
for others rather than moaning about
what I don't have in my life.*

"Age is an issue of mind over matter.
If you don't mind, it doesn't matter."

—*Mark Twain*

"How does it feel to be 80?" I asked my Great Aunt Emma. "Really, no different than any other age," she replied, "unless I look in the mirror, or try to do something strenuous. On the inside, I feel exactly like I have at every age before now. The mirror tells me otherwise, of course, and I know when I can no longer chop wood or something. But other than that, I'm the same as I always was." That encounter was many years ago, when she was "old" to my youthful mind.

Today, as I am 63 and feeling more "old" than youthful, I often think of how true her words were and embrace them as my own. I do not feel any different unless I pass a mirror or try to do something strenuous. At the present time, my body needs more exercise, and it is carrying too much weight for good health, but those are habits that I can change. I can assist my physical body to be stronger and healthier by becoming more mindful of the choices I make. My mind and spirit are young. The choices I make each day with them are good ones. Practicing better habits with my body will make it as youthful as my mind and spirit. How I feel, at 63, 73, 83, or beyond is up to me. I'll just avoid looking in any mirrors, thank you.

—*Deborah Ann Hagen*

*I pray for the discipline to take care of my body,
mind, and spirit, even when I feel lazy!*

> "Learning to live from conscious intention
> rather than from habit energy and past conditioning
> is the path of awakening."
>
> —*Fred Eppsteiner*

As we learn to practice mindfulness, we are not going to be successful all the time. Our minds will still wander. It takes time to be aware of the present moment and the thoughts we are having in the present moment. It takes time to realize our reactions come from habitual ways of thinking and that we can change how we respond.

We may have spent all our previous years being unaware that we have any control over our thoughts. Our minds have gone to our past and to our future, rarely letting us stay in the present moment. Our minds have told us so many things that aren't true, such as we aren't good enough or we'll never be a success. Our thoughts have scared us by telling us all the things we have to fear as we grow old.

Gradually, as we practice mindfulness, this awareness will deepen and we will be freer and freer of our past conditioning.

God is helping me let go of my old, negative,
and self-defeating habits. My intention is to live in
the present moment and this fills me with joy.

"Surround yourself only with those people
who are going to lift you higher."
—*Oprah Winfrey*

Studies have shown that when we spend time with positive, supportive, and loving people, we will be happier, more content, and more likely to live longer. Daniel Amen, M.D., who is a clinical neuroscientist, psychiatrist, and brain imaging expert, writes, "When you spend time with negative or hostile people, you tend to feel tense, anxious, upset, and sick, and you increase your stress hormones. Increases in the stress hormone cortisol can disrupt neurons in the hippocampus, one of the main memory centers in the brain."

Check out who you spend time with. Do they support you and give you positive messages? Do you feel encouraged by them or do they put you down? Are your friends positive or negative? Are they sarcastic? Many people think sarcasm is funny. It actually comes from a Greek word meaning tearing flesh.

It's important to take a good look at your friends and make changes if you find they fit in the negative category.

In one detailed health study, 10,000 men were asked, "Does your wife show you her love?" Ten years later, those who had answered yes showed fewer ulcers and less chest pain and lived longer!

*I deserve friends who lift my spirits, just
as I lift the spirits of my friends.*

"To be yourself in a world that is constantly
trying to make you something else is
the greatest accomplishment."

—*Ralph Waldo Emerson*

*It feels so good to let go of all my "shoulds":
everything I think I should be, everything I do
to get people to like me, and just be
me for the rest of my life!*

"They say that age is all in your mind. The trick is
keeping it from creeping down into your body."

—Author unknown

I have to be constantly mindful about what my body can and
cannot do. Although I am very fortunate to be physically
quite able, I do have chronic back issues related to some disc
deterioration. I have to always be aware of how my body feels
and make a mindful judgment about whether I can or should
do whatever physical thing presents itself. I must "Think before
doing." Overdoing even simple things can send me straight to
the recliner and the ice-pack. More difficult things like getting
down on hands and knees can get downright funny when I try to
get up. Then I yell to my spouse, "Rogerrrrrrr, help!"

It's not only the physical body that requires mindfulness; it's
the mind. Things happen, such as walking into a room on some
errand then forgetting why I entered that room; driving myself
to an appointment or the market and finding myself halfway to
my daughter's house instead, and having to turn around.

I can't operate on auto-pilot as much as I used to. I really have
to be mindful of what I am doing. It is when I act habitually,
unmindfully that I am most apt to get into some kind of trouble.
Aging mindfully means aging more safely and being healthier in
mind and body. You might call it "preventive medicine."

—Mary Bell

*Today I am being more mindful of everything
I am doing, taking care to embrace my limitations without
self-pity or regret, but with the peace that comes
from accepting the reality of each moment.*

good to know

Studies show that gardeners have a lower incidence of
heart disease and osteoporosis than nongardeners.

Mindful gardening . . . what a treat! Keeping our awareness
on what we are doing in each moment. Smelling and feeling the soil, the flowers, the water. Being one with the plants.
Feeling a part of the earth. Being aware of the muscles we are
using when we dig into the earth.

The joy of cutting a stem from the bush and bringing it in the
house to enjoy the flower. The joy of planting a seed and seeing
it sprout. The joy of turning the corner and seeing your garden in
front of your house. The joy of seeing a plant from the window
or in our room when we wake in the morning. The joy of feeling
the sun on our bodies, the breeze against our hair and clothing.

Being one with nature brings me great joy.

"Study spiritual works, apply your learnings
to improve your life, practice prayer and meditation,
and express universal love through service to others,
and your evolution will not only enlighten
you but add years to your life."

—*Dr. Maoshing Ni*

Meditators, positive people, optimists, people with faith, spiritual people are happier people. The good news is that science is now proving what people have always known about what makes our aging healthy and happy. Science is showing us that with practice we can change. We can rewire our brain. So if we have tended to be on the depressive, pessimistic, low self-esteem side by nature, we don't have to stay this way.

There is so much we can do to increase our chances of living with joy as we grow older. Expressing universal love and generosity to others gives us an immediate, positive change in our brain and in our emotions. Praying and meditating brings us inner peace and increases our immune system. These are just a few of the things we can do. Why would we want to wait?

*Today I am making an intention to add to my life
one new routine that will bring me joy.*

"Music making is linked to a number of
health benefits for older adults. Research shows
that making music can lower blood pressure,
decrease heart rate, reduce stress, and lessen anxiety and
depression. There is also increasing evidence that
making music enhances the immunological response,
which enables us to fight viruses."

—*Dr. Suzanne Hanser*

Latest studies show that slow, soothing music is good for your health while fast, stimulating music is not. Calming classical music enhances cognitive functions such as memory, concentration, and reasoning skills. It also boosts the immune system, lowers blood pressure, relaxes muscle tension, regulates stress hormones, elevates mood, and increases endurance.

There is also an increasing focus in the medical community on the need to keep the brain as healthy as the body. Dr. Hanser tells us that music helps to make the empty-nest and retirement years fun and worthwhile and is also about preventing debilitating dementias such as Alzheimer's disease. Music making has the potential to do both.

*I am staying mindful of all the latest research
and exploring what feels right for me. There is so much
I can do to find joy as I grow older.*

"When you arise in the morning, think of what a precious privilege it is to be alive—to breathe, to think, to enjoy, to love."

—*Marcus Aurelius*

There are at least two powerful reasons for us to move slowly when we wake up in the morning and not just plunge into activity. The first one is spiritual. When we begin our morning with prayer and meditation, we are connecting with the God of our understanding. We are making a decision to follow a spiritual path and to come from a place of peace and love.

I have found that reading inspirational words brings me to a very quiet, spiritual place, setting the stage for my day.

Journaling is also wonderful to do. Simply writing what is going on, expressing something bothersome to you so that it is not kept inside and festering.

Writing affirmations, or positive statements for something you would like to change or achieve, can also be done in the morning. Creating an intention for how you would like to live this day is also a wonderful habit to get into.

It has been found that people have more strokes and heart attacks between the times of 6 AM and noon. Most people get up and go directly into their daily activities. Their body experiences a sudden increase in body temperature, blood pressure, and heart rate. This creates a strain on weak artery walls.

Remember, 20 minutes of meditation is equivalent to two hours sleep, so by getting up a little earlier to meditate, pray, or doing other spiritual activities, you won't be as tired. You will be ready to experience your day with a healthier body, a clear mind, and an open heart.

I begin each day with prayer and meditation, my quiet time
with God. It is my special time to prepare for my day,
filling my soul with peace and love and joy.

When I was a child I really wanted to have a dog. I prayed for one and nothing happened. I questioned if there was a God and later, in college, with long nights of intellectual and, so I thought, deep discussions, I became an agnostic. Maybe there is. Maybe there isn't. And we'll never know.

Over the years I became addicted to alcohol and it was suggested that I pray to have my desire removed. It was also suggested that since I didn't believe in God, I insert an extra "o" in the word God and pray to the power of good and to the power of love. This worked and I have not had a drink in many years. I now know there is a power greater than myself. There is no need to define it.

I like Dr. Maoshing Ni's definition of faith. He writes, "Faith is a belief in a higher power, universal order or force behind creation that some call God. Faith allows one to find peace within, to accept what is and to reconcile the differences between one's expectations and reality." Whatever this power is for you, whether it be the Buddha within, Supreme Being, Spirit, or Allah, does not matter. What is important is that research has shown that more people with faith in a higher power live longer and are healthier.

It is a joy to know that with my faith I am happier, healthier, and have more freedom and peace in my life.

"The mind is the source of all experience, and
by changing the direction of the mind, we can change
the quality of everything we experience."

—A Buddhist teaching

The Buddha taught this 2,600 years ago and scientists are now proving this to be true. By changing our thoughts we change our brains and thus change how we feel.

I used to think that some people were just born positive and others negative, and they had to stay that way. I did not think it possible to change. I was very quiet and painfully shy and in my midthirties became very depressed. After becoming a daily meditator, this changed so that I am no longer depressed. A miracle! I am a new person. When the old me walked down the street and someone was coming in my direction, I would lower my eyes so I would not have contact. Now I smile and might even say hello. I feel good about meeting a new person.

What would you like to change today? What do you think will make you happy? What behavior would you like to let go of, such as impatience or anger? What new characteristic would you like to have, such as patience or forgiveness?

Mindfulness can give us the ability to make these changes. By being mindful, we can stop and catch ourselves when we are thinking negative, unpleasant thoughts and we can practice changing them. This might not happen in 24 hours, but over time, you actually can change the way you think and thus the way you feel.

*Today I am learning to be mindful of all my thoughts,
becoming aware of how they make me feel, and practicing turning
around negative thoughts into ones of compassion and love.*

"May everyone have the food they need,
the happiness they seek, and may they attain relief
from the suffering of a dissatisfied mind."

—*Sasha T. Loring*

It is very human to want to avoid pain and suffering and to feel only happiness and joy. We find things or activities that make us feel good and then we want more and more. Food, sex, shopping, alcohol, and drugs are just a few of the places where we turn to take away our unpleasant feelings. This is where addictions begin. Addictions create stress in our bodies, which harms our immune systems and causes us many problems, mentally, physically and spiritually we grow older.

Sasha T. Loring points us to a wonderful way to stop our cravings. She suggests that when we are longing for something, we name it, just as we name our thoughts in meditation. For example, if it is food we want, we name the feeling, and then we say, "May all beings have enough to eat."

Perhaps you want to buy clothing and can't afford the item. You might say, "May everyone have enough clothes to keep them warm."

She suggests we redirect our wanting mind into one of generosity and caring. When we bring our awareness to our feelings of craving, and stop and breathe, we don't have to act out without thinking. We don't have to react. We can pause, realize what we are considering, and then offer the object of our craving to others who might need it in a healthy way.

*I am bringing awareness to my "wanting mind" today and
finding ways of compassion and generosity to relieve it.*

"To age gracefully means to let nature take
its course while doing everything in our power to
delay the onset of age-related disease, or, in other words,
to live as long and as well as possible . . ."

—*Andrew Weil, M.D.*

A number of people answered a questionnaire I put out on aging. The answers came from people in their 40s to their 70s. One question was, "Do you have any fears around aging?" The results were varied, yet there were some recurring themes. One was financial. The second was being lonely or socially isolated. The third was all that comes with becoming mentally and physically disabled. My fears included: "I am afraid I won't be able to support myself," "I don't want to lose my independence," "I don't want to be a burden to others," "I don't want to be put in a nursing home and lose my independence," and "I don't want to be at the 'mercy' of others."

One woman summed up an answer that can help us all:

At 68, I believe the train is already coming down the track full speed ahead and there is no stopping it. It's too late to buy another ticket and the train is going too fast to jump off. Anything that could have been done to prepare financially for seniorhood is a moot point. My job is to accept what I have now that I'm a senior. I'm willing to continue working and know I will have to do so for as long as I am physically and mentally able to do so. I am very conscious of living within my means and not accumulating debt. In the final analysis, I am trusting my Higher Power to help me work it out.

Today I am doing everything I can to prepare myself for my future.
I am trusting my Higher Power to take it from there.

good news

Mindfulness can help us calm our fears around aging. The more we meditate, the more aware we become of our thoughts. We can listen to our negative thoughts that lead to our fears, and rather than beat ourselves up for having them, or believing them, we can gently turn them around to a positive affirmation. It has been proven that positive people live longer, are healthier, and live a happier life.

Affirmations are positive statements we can use to make our intentions a reality. You can look at your own fears around aging or choose one from the following list. The important thing here is that you say and write them ten times a day for twenty-one days. Say them "as if" you believe them. Say them with feeling and passion you can change a negative, fearful attitude to one that is positive:

I let go of all my fears of aging today and turn them over to God.

I feel safe in knowing that all my needs are being met as I move through life.

I have everything I need today.

I am taking care of myself mentally, physically, and spiritually.

God is helping me turn my fear into faith.

"Mindfulness is a particular kind of awareness,
which is purposeful, focused, curious, and rooted in our
moment-by-moment experience. With mindfulness we
purposefully observe our experience as it takes place,
including any pain that may be present."

—Bodhipaksa

Aging brings its own aches and pains. Our natural reaction is to tighten up and do whatever we can to avoid or push away pain. This creates more stress and increases our pain. Our first answer might be to take pain pills, alcohol, or drugs to avoid our suffering.

As we practice mindfulness, we learn to be with whatever is in the present moment. We might be sitting meditating and thoughts come in. We label them "thoughts," or "thinking," or "planning." We accept them, and by allowing them to be there, they fade away.

We can deal with pain in the same manner and suffer less. We can be curious about the pain. An attitude of curiosity allows us to let go of our resistance. We can pay attention to the pain and see that it is an ever-changing variety of sensations.

Rather than thinking, "I can't stand this pain. When will it ever end?" we can be aware if the pain is hot or cold, tingling or throbbing. Simply breathing in to our pain can soften and lighten it.

Doctors tell us that pain is our body's natural way of letting us know that something might be wrong. Mindfulness does not take the place of medical treatment but it can help us to deal with our pain and make it our friend, rather than our enemy.

*Today I am being gentle and mindful of
any pain I might feel, accepting it as a part of life and
not something I need to fear or get rid of.*

> "How foolish to think one could slam the door
> in the face of Age. Much better to be polite and
> gracious and ask him to lunch in advance."
>
> —*Noel Coward*

On one hand I was thrilled to turn 62 years old. I could now get senior discounts! And at the same time I was equally thrilled when the cashier would look at me with a smile and say I didn't look old enough to be a senior.

I had fun with these reactions for quite a few years until the day came when no one questioned my senior discount. In fact, the first time someone said they had already given me one without my asking, I was devastated. *What?* I thought. *They think I look old enough now? What happened? I must be looking my age.* I felt depressed. Disappointed. I could never get that feeling back. It was over.

Soon I accepted the truth. I did look my age and that was that. And when I lost weight I looked even older. My chubby cheeks no longer hid my wrinkles. More acceptance. More getting used to the reality of aging.

I am very grateful that our Creator is very kind and does not let our changes show from hour to hour or even day by day, but very gradually. It doesn't happen that we see ten new wrinkles in one day. Our appearance changes very slowly. We might not be aware of the gradual change until we look in the mirror one day and say, "Oh my God, when did this happen?"

I pray for acceptance, humor, grace, and gratitude
as I grow older, one day at a time.

"Aging is not just decay, you know. It's growth.
It's more than the negative that you're going to die;
it's the positive that you understand you're going to die,
and that you live a better life because of it."

—*Mitch Albom*, Tuesdays with Morrie

We've probably all read stories about people who know they have six months or twelve months or two weeks to live, and they stop to figure out all the things they want to do before they die. I enjoyed *The Bucket List*, a movie about two terminally ill cancer patients who decide to break out of the hospital and live their last days to the fullest. They made what they called their bucket list and set out to do each thing on it. Fortunately, one of them had enough money to make that possible.

We don't have to wait until we are terminally ill or old or even until we have more money. We can make our own bucket list now and do all the things we would like to do but have put off. Of course, we have to make our list reasonable and within our means. If all your dreams are too expensive, make a new list!

Not everything on your list has to cost money. Perhaps you have always wanted to read to the blind or play the flute or write your memoirs. Perhaps there is someone you have harmed and put off making amends. Perhaps you have wanted to learn to line dance or feed the homeless. You could set up a schedule to do something you have always wanted to do each month or three months or year. But don't put them off any longer. We never know how much time we have left, so we should live fully each day.

Today I am going deep into my heart to discover what will give me the greatest satisfactions in life. And I am going to do them!

Sitting quietly,
breathing in and breathing out
I feel softer and
more relaxed.
I am aware of the tension
leaving my body
as I breathe in peace
and breathe out tension.
I can imagine
healing energy
flowing through
all the parts
of my body.
I know I'm more than my pain.
I can focus on my breath
and
feel
peace.

I had a wonderful conversation with Ruth Eppsteiner, who is almost 94 years old. I admire her for her warmth, gentleness, openness, and loving ways. I asked her if she would tell me to what she attributes all these qualities, and her answer was very enlightening.

She felt very lucky as she was always surrounded by loving and devoted people. She said she was lucky to have always had the attitude of the cup always being half full rather than half empty.

When she was exposed to mindfulness, she took to it right away and began to apply its teaching to her life. It expanded her tolerance and she has let go of all judgments. It's helped her with her memory, and she believes she is even a better bridge player because of it.

Ruth said that the teachings are so simple, and they have gotten her through all kinds of ups and downs. They include acceptance, knowing that everything is impermanent, and that nothing is a big deal. In addition. Ruth eats a healthy diet and practices yoga regularly.

And she is full of gratitude.

The practice of mindfulness is simple. The word "practice" means doing something over and over again so that we can get better at it.

Ruth, at 93 years old, is a powerful example.

I am placing mindfulness on my daily priority list
and find joy in practicing it formally in the morning and
as best as I can during the rest of the day.

"A problem shared is a problem cut in half."

—Unknown sage

It was February and I had just returned from a five-day silent retreat, where I couldn't do any writing. In two weeks I was to lead a weekend retreat and had to spend time preparing for it. In three weeks I was scheduled for a knee replacement, and I knew there would be at least a few days when I wouldn't be able to write.

This book was due in two months. I thought that I would never be able to finish it on time. I meditated. I prayed. I turned the book over to God. I tried to change my thoughts. I focused on my breath. I told myself to be in today, in this moment, in this breath. I was stressed and that upset me even more because I thought I could handle stressful times. The one thing I hadn't done was to share my concerns with another person.

Just then, Joanne, one of my meditation teachers, returned my call. I poured it out the second she asked how I was.

"Breathe," she said. "Instead of worrying, write another page."

I had invited her to write a page for the book and when I mentioned that she still had plenty of time to write it, she laughed and said, "Tell that to yourself."

She told me what I already knew but still needed to hear again.

There are times when all we know isn't enough. We need to share what is going on inside of us. We need to release our feelings and thus release our stress. We need to share our struggles and admit we are not perfect.

That is one of the ways we can find joy.

There is such freedom when I allow myself to let another human being really get to know me, with all my imperfections.

"Sometimes, in the process of trying to deny
that things are always changing, we lose our sense of
the sacredness of life. We tend to forget that we are
part of the natural scheme of things."

—*Pema Chödrön*

As we age there are bound to be some days that simply feel more difficult than others. There is no law that says we have to push ourselves. Expectations about how we should feel can cause us great suffering.

Maybe we no longer can play sports at the same intensity and skill we did when we were younger. Maybe the days we could be active for 16 hours become more like 12 hours or 10 hours or even 6 hours. The harder we try to be what we used to be, the greater we suffer. It's so much better to enjoy what we are doing, rather than trying to go beyond what we are capable of doing and feeling sorry for ourselves.

For some of us, our finances decline as well as our physical strength. We might not be able to live as free a life as we once did. We might have to live on a tighter budget or work longer than we expected. Here, too, accepting the reality of our situation leads to happiness rather than suffering. The "poor me's" pull us down. Gratitude for what we do have lifts our spirits.

Today I am being mindful of my strengths and limitations.
I am living in my own true reality and this gives me great joy!

"Rather than viewing the second half of life as
a time of progressive deterioration in body and mind,
we see aging as an opportunity for greater wisdom,
love, creativity, meaning, joy and increased mental
and physical capacity. More people than ever
are living into their eighties, nineties and beyond
with sound bodies and clear minds."

—*Deepak Chopra, M.D.*

We have come so far with our medical knowledge and treatment that the average life span has expanded more than 60 years! In the Roman Empire it was just 28 years. In the beginning of the twentieth century for those born in the Western world it was 49 years. Now the fastest growing segment of the American population is over 90.

There is so much we can do to help these expanded years be years of richness and joy by taking care of ourselves mentally, physically, and spiritually. Mindfulness meditation, continuing to learn, staying active socially, growing spiritually, and having a life of purpose helping others are the major things on which we can concentrate. Making an intention each day to grow in these areas will not give us a 100 percent guarantee that we will be healthy and happy as we live to be 100 years old, but it will improve our chances that this is possible.

*I have every intention of living a rich and meaningful life.
I pray for the strength, determination, discipline, and
steadfastness to do all that is in my power to make this come true.*

> "To forgive is to set a prisoner free and
> discover the prisoner was you."
>
> *—Author unknown*

When my father was 90 years old we had to put him in a nursing home. He had been living independently in his own apartment, but he drank too much. One day fell down and broke his ankle and he could no longer take care of himself.

I was going through the motions of doing the right thing, doing what a daughter does for one's parent. I knew I was being cold and distant. I could not hide my feelings, hard as I tried, as I had not yet forgiven him for his years of drinking and verbal abuse. As much as I knew that forgiveness was necessary, I wasn't ready.

His body was bent and he was leaning over on his walker as we entered the home with him. He looked around and seemed to get stronger for a moment. His shoulders straightened and he said, "Well, if they can do it, I guess I can, too."

In that instant my heart opened and I remembered my father as a younger man, a man who had given me courage and inspiration when I was much younger. It was the beginning of the road to forgiveness, the road that would eventually take me to a place of love, understanding, compassion, and respect.

For us to live with joy in our hearts as we grow older, we can't hold on to any anger or resentments. We have to be willing to let go of everything that is blocking us from feeling love.

Today I turn everything over to the God of my understanding,
holding on to nothing that keeps me from joy.

"I hope you will discover and enjoy the benefits that aging
can bring: wisdom, depth of character, the smoothing out
of what is rough and harsh, the evaporation of what is
inconsequential, and the concentration of true worth."

—Andrew Weil, M.D.

This is the last day of our year. Tomorrow begins an entirely
new year on the calendar but in truth is really nothing more
than a continuation of today. Just as we age, one day flowing into
the next and into the next, until we become aware we are older.

Each day is as important as another day. We can make an
intention today that we will do all we can to be the person we
were meant to be. We don't have to let another day go by without
living to our fullest potential.

Mindfulness can show us the way. It can help us live a loving,
compassionate and purpose-filled life. Ralph Waldo Emerson
says it beautifully:

To laugh often and much, to win the respect of intelligent people
and the affection of children, to appreciate beauty, to find the best
in others, to leave the world a bit better, whether by a healthy child,
a garden, or a redeemed social condition; to know even one life has
breathed easier because you have lived. This is to have succeeded.

Today I am filled with joy,
knowing that all I have to do is to begin
my day with prayer and meditation.

Reflections

Reflections

Reflections

Reflections

in spite of getting older

Reflections

living in the
"now"

_____

_____

_____

_____

_____

_____

_____

_____

_____

_____

_____

_____

_____

_____

_____

_____

_____

_____

More Great Books from Ruth Fishel

Code #0677 • Paperback • $12.95

Solve your problems by creating your own personal
affirmations and achieve inner peace.

Living Light as a Feather

How to Find Joy in Every Day and a Purpose in Every Problem

Ruth Fishel
Author of *Time for Joy*

Code #1576 • Paperback • $11.95

Find the tools and motivation
you need to take the first step
to having a joyful heart.

If everyone took time each day for one thoughtful act, the world would be a much better place.

Time for Thoughtfulness
A Daily Guide to Filling the World
with Love, Care and Compassion

By Ruth Fishel
Illustrations by Bonny Van de Kamp

Code #3227 • Paperback • $7.95

The Journey Within

NOW

A Spiritual
Path To Recovery

Ruth Fishel

Code #4419 • Paperback • $8.95

A spiritual path to recovery will lead you to the place where healing occurs from within.

By the Bestselling Author of *Time for Joy*

TAKE TIME
FOR
YOURSELF

RUTH FISHEL

MEDITATIVE MOMENTS FOR
HEALTHY LIVING

Illustrations by Bonny Van de Kamp

Code 3685 • Paperback • $8.95

Heal your wounded spirit and empower
your life with this captivating book.